"Anyone on the spectrum who has experienced a suicide in their family—a crisis which involved the police or other authorities, medical emergencies, and the like—can relate to this book. Similarly, this is a book the emergency service providers should read too because those in the helping professions aren't actually helping us when they use their usual methods. But, this is not a clinical how-to. This is a detailed, emotional, and vivid account, almost a play-by-play, of the events which transpired from the moment of that fateful phone call. Behind the events, the physical movements, are the thoughts and reactions that only another person on the autism spectrum can truly understand, but everyone should try. A heart-wrenching, honest account of the kind of experience that no one should have to go through, but, unfortunately many of us do."

—*Rudy Simone, author of* The A to Z of
ASDs: Aunt Aspie's Guide to Life

"The excellent and much-needed book deals with the specific issues—emotional and practical—faced by people on the autism spectrum when a loved one completes suicide. Written from a personal, lived experience perspective, this sensitive and valuable book validates the experience of readers and helps them to manage what is essentially unmanageable."

—*Jeanette Purkis, autism self-advocate and author of* The Guide
to Good Mental Health on the Autism Spectrum

"Lisa compassionately, courageously, and incisively offers the reader the wisdom and learnings she earned through experiencing the tragic loss of her husband to suicide. I can highly recommend this book to anyone on the autism spectrum bereaved by suicide and to their support network. The reader will discover distilled wisdom and strategies for each part of their own journey."

—*Dr. Michelle S. Garnett, Clinic Director and Clinical
Psychologist, Minds & Hearts Clinic, Brisbane, Australia*

LIVING THROUGH
SUICIDE LOSS

——— WITH AN———
Autistic Spectrum Disorder
(ASD)

*An Insider Guide for Individuals,
Family, Friends, and Professional
Responders*

LISA MORGAN M.ED.

Foreword by Dr. Carla Stumpf Patton

Jessica Kingsley *Publishers*
London and Philadelphia

First published in 2017
by Jessica Kingsley Publishers
73 Collier Street
London N1 9BE, UK
and
400 Market Street, Suite 400
Philadelphia, PA 19106, USA

www.jkp.com

Library of Congress Cataloging in Publication Data
A CIP catalog record for this book is available from the Library of Congress

British Library Cataloguing in Publication Data
A CIP catalogue record for this book is available from the British Library

ISBN 978 1 78592 729 4
eISBN 978 1 78450 400 7

Printed and bound in Great Britain

MIX
Paper from
responsible sources
FSC® C013056

This book is dedicated to Paul, my best friend for 30 years, my husband, and the father of my children, a kind, witty, extremely intelligent man whose life was stolen by an undiagnosed mental illness. May you rest in peace.

(7/12/1961–6/24 /2015)

Contents

Foreword

It is nearly impossible to find someone who has not been impacted by suicide in some way—be it through a personal loss of a loved one, friend, or colleague, or perhaps by caring for someone else who has struggled with suicidal thoughts or survived a suicide attempt. Perhaps you know someone who has battled depression, addiction, or posttraumatic stress, or perhaps the person is yourself. Maybe you or someone else who you know has been impacted in some of these ways, or perhaps a story you have heard about, such as a celebrity suicide, has impacted you and you want to understand more. By some chance, maybe you are fortunate enough to not have known the devastation of suicide, but you want to be proactive and supportive to those who have. Regardless of the reason, by reading *Living Through Suicide Loss with an Autistic Spectrum Disorder (ASD)*, you will learn more about how the lives of suicide loss survivors are impacted.

As a licensed psychotherapist specializing in suicide bereavement and traumatic loss, I have walked along such survivors living through suicide loss for over two decades now, and have a professional career dedicated to helping families coping with the tragedy of suicide and the unfathomable transition as they adjust to their "new normal" in the absence of the "physical" presence of their loved done. What does this have to do with my understanding of ASD, you might ask? A large part of my career was spent working in a school that specialized in students (and their families) with varying learning differences, many of whom were on the spectrum. I eventually came to meet my then coworker, Lisa, where, in time and when she felt secure, she eventually shared more about her own personal experiences of living with Asperger's. With a lot of effort, time, and trust, our relationship as colleagues eventually evolved into a deeper friendship, and is now more like family, living through the many things that families do. Little did we know when we first met, that in time, we would come to share a deeper connection; something far darker and more painful than most people can imagine and what Lisa will elaborate on in her own story throughout this book.

As friends often do, Lisa and I both shared important parts of our lives with one another in hopes of building upon our friendship. I shared how I had become a military widow in 1994 at a young age, losing my spouse, a Marine Corps Drill Instructor, to suicide just a few days before our child was born. She knew I later remarried a widower who was also a U.S. Marine, how we blended our military families and had rebuilt our lives over the years. Lisa and I would often discuss how this impacted my family and how our children had coped with loss. She knew about the struggles of my deceased loved one, and my involvement in supporting families surviving suicide loss. We also had many discussions about Lisa's family, what it had been like for a person growing up with Asperger's, and some of the struggles (and gifts) that come from living with ASD. Lisa and I had endless conversations about these issues and always mutually supported one another. After several years of building our friendship, our worlds would converge again on another level of profound loss—the day when Lisa found that her husband Paul died and their family became survivors of suicide loss.

Knowing first-hand how everything changed in those moments, I rushed to my friend's side. Her family had already become like our family and her kids were like my own kids. I knew that nothing could fix this—and that no words, no actions, no gifts, and no casseroles would ease the pain. I had the unfortunate benefit of having had first-hand accounts on what she could expect. In the early days clouded by shock, disbelief, and trauma, it didn't matter so much about what I would say, because the shock and trauma would likely mean that Lisa would not recall much of what we discussed anyway, and was more so about what I would do, so I just did some of the basic things that friends and family can do to help survivors living through suicide loss: Be mentally and physically present. Follow through and show up. Listen more and talk less. Do not abandon them. Love, unconditionally and without judgment.

Suicidal behaviors or thinking (or suicidality) when left silenced by myths and stigma, left unattended, left unaddressed, and left on its own, can prove to be fatal. In its wake, it leaves a path of destruction for all of those in the life of the person who has died. Death in general, can be a difficult subject to discuss for many, and in the case of suicide, it can often entail graphic and traumatic details that people are not equipped to discuss. Many times, people are not sure what to do or say, or they might even cast judgment and ridicule upon the deceased (or the surviving family members), which only contributes to the surviving families feeling more isolated. This is a time when the bereaved family will need unconditional and unwavering support more than ever.

It is impossible to understand what survivors of suicide loss experience without understanding more about the nature of suicide and how, why, and when it occurs, and this is a large part of what survivors of loss are left wondering more about. There can be an elevated risk of suicidal thoughts and behaviors in people with ASD, but more importantly, issues such as secondary depression and suicidality are preventable through timely diagnosis, strong supports and treatments, and improved mental health care. Most people considering suicide do not simply want to die; rather, they see no other alternatives to solve their problems or to relieve their pain, and death may begin to feel like the only option. Often, people who are considering suicide think they are doing others a favor, or that those around them will be better off without them, or that they are resolving the crisis by ending their lives. They feel the situation is hopeless and beyond help, but what they don't realize is how the suicide does not end the problem(s), because the emotional crisis is passed to all of the grieving survivors who are left behind to make sense of their loved one's death. In fact, a family history of suicide deaths (of loved ones) can actually raise the potential risk of suicide for surviving family members. This is one more important reason why professional supports in form of counseling are highly effective in helping people cope with such losses and therefore reducing possible risks.

After suicide loss, families are left with a life that has been leveled to the ground by mass destruction and where they are now tasked with the foreign concept of rebuilding a foundation in the midst of their grief when the elements of trust and control have been shaken. For families who were present, witnessed, or exposed to the elements of the death (as in Lisa's case), there can be added layers of trauma (many of which are rooted in sensory issues) which is an issue beyond grief that can leave complex, lingering effects of acute stress, and possibly emerge into posttraumatic stress for some individuals.

Every family will mourn their loss differently and each member within the family will react, communicate, and grieve in their own unique way. After a suicide loss, it is critical for families to reconstruct a new foundation based on healthy coping skills. They will need to work diligently on communication skills and seeking outside help in the form of counseling when needed. They will have to work together to reconnect with one another and their surrounding support system. In time, it is hoped that they will regain a new found sense of control, and eventually come to feel empowered that they have choices in the direction of healing for their family. With her husband's death, Lisa is living through the loss, continuing on the journey, and courageously sharing the story of how she is healing. *Living Through Suicide Loss with an Autistic Spectrum Disorder (ASD)* will be valuable in offering hope, encouragement, and healing to you the reader, and to all those who you love and support.

Dr. Carla Stumpf Patton, EdD,
LMHC, NCC, FT, CCTP

Acknowledgments

My heart has been warmed many times by the kindness of others during this season in my life.

I appreciate everyone who has supported me, stayed with me, left me, and loved me—without all of that I would not be who I am today.

I have a special place in my heart for the people who were there with me through it all:

My four children, Rachel, Benjamin, Levi, and Gabriel—my reasons to live, laugh, love, and heal.

Carla, my cherished friend, there from before the beginning, with loving, caring support—she saved my life.

My sister Terri came from the north and helped the boys and me to happily forget for a while.

My mother Grace prayed for me every day.

Alison, my fun friend, who showed me I could still enjoy life in the midst of the sadness.

Josh, the best friend and role model the boys could ever have and a true friend to me.

Elaine, a new friend, was there to listen to me when I needed to talk.

My treasured friend Justine has been there, with compassion and down-to-earth wisdom, who also read and edited every chapter with honest feedback and helpful suggestions.

My faithful and loving Lord, who truly lived out Hebrews 13:5b in my life when He said *I will never leave you, nor forsake you.*

Preface

This book is about the unique challenges an adult diagnosed with Asperger's syndrome (AS) faces in the aftermath of a loved one completing suicide. The term for a person whose life is affected by the suicide of a loved one is called a "survivor of suicide loss."

And it really does feel like you have survived a devastating assault on your life; every aspect of your life changes. You change. You are now missing an important person who was a huge part of your life, and they left by choice, which severely complicates the grieving process. Depending on who you lost, you are either grieving as a parent, a spouse, a sibling, a friend, or from one of a myriad of other relationships that have all left behind different situations to grieve through. Each circumstance leaves a gaping hole in the life of the survivor of suicide loss, the common thread being that the people left behind all have to pick up the pieces and move forward in life, without their loved one.

The unique difficulties a person with an ASD (an Aspie or a person with AS – terms most adults on the spectrum call themselves even though the official terminology has changed) experiences during the time following the suicide of a loved one are right in the areas of their lives where they most likely have always struggled—relationships.

For some reason usually unknown to the Aspie, an important relationship is lost after a death, especially suicide. Just when a person needs the friends and family who are closest to them in their lives the most, they lose them.

For a person living with AS, these relationships are, in so many ways, a devastating loss that can't be recovered. Most likely, an Aspie, with their social skills deficits, has put enormous energy for a very long time into building and keeping a relationship, so losing it means there's just no one else. Absolutely no one else, meaning it would be extraordinary for an Aspie to have the energy, social skills, desire, or even ability to start a new friendship while experiencing all the emotions and grief inherent to a survivor of suicide loss. An Aspie is in the worst state possible to even begin to think about starting a new friendship, so they end up feeling alone to face the worst, loneliest, most confusing time in their lives.

And it's so often more than one relationship the Aspie loses, which compounds the grief and guilt already consuming them. So the Aspie is facing the seemingly impossible task of funeral arrangements, bio-hazard clean-up, mortgages, IRAs, bank accounts, nobody cooperating, being executor of the will, dealing with creditors, lawyers, moving house, grieving children, going through a loved one's belongings, going back to work, relentless phone calls with uncaring machines and/or uncaring people, and, lastly, their own grief while *feeling* alone and disconnected.

Then, the punishing guilt of having said or done the wrong thing, to either the person who completed suicide or the friends who left, is heartbreaking. All of these scenarios come while an Aspie could be struggling with uncontrollable anxiety, extreme sensory overload, receptive and expressive language problems, depression, and deep emotional pain, feeling all alone. It is truly a time of change, challenge, and having the strength you never knew you had to walk through the aftermath of a loved one completing suicide.

The purpose of this book is to explain all the complications, miscommunications, losses, vulnerabilities, and unexpected situations that have happened to me as I have walked and am walking through the aftermath of the completed suicide of my husband, Paul. My hope is that this book will validate the added difficulties an Aspie struggles with due to the fundamental differences defining a person with AS. My goal is that this book will serve as a guide and as a friend when other friends have walked away and left you to wrap up the life you knew and begin a new one on your own. A new life that you never asked for, never wanted, and don't understand is frightening, and along with all that, it feels like you are taking the first steps into a new life alone, lost, and completely confused.

The content of this book is the story of my walk through the aftermath of the completed suicide of my husband. As I write this, it's only been 11 months since his body was found, so my journey is not yet finished. Still, I have enough to share already to write a book about it.

Would you believe me if I told you the grief and/or guilt, although exceptionally painful, wasn't the worst part of my experience? It's true. The worst part for me was being misunderstood, miscommunications with people, broken relationships, handling the finances, taking care of my kids in their pain, the sensory issues, and all the confusion in my life.

There are clear reasons why all the things I just listed were so difficult. The first is that I was living in a world where I counted on the rules of etiquette, which I now realize most people just use as suggestions, so there are no real ground rules on saying or doing the right thing.

The second reason is that each interaction was a different form of social situation that I had to work through, figure out, and do right, all while working with extremely slow processing speeds, hindered receptive and expressive language abilities, overloaded sensory issues, and having no choice on whether I wanted to have those interactions or not. Things just had to be done when they had to be done.

I'm going to be pointing out where the two worlds of neurotypicals (people not diagnosed with an ASD) and Aspies collided in ways that caused the extra difficulties I experienced. I'm pointing them out in the hope that anyone who reads this will come away with a new understanding that some people experience situations vastly different from others. I will point them out as I go along to make it even clearer and easier to understand.

I would also like to mention that not all of the difficulties listed above are only experienced by people on the spectrum. There are many who find themselves in this same situation for whatever reason—it doesn't really matter, but they, too, are struggling to keep their head above water in the muck and mire of the aftermath of being a survivor of suicide loss. This book is for them too. No one who is a survivor of suicide loss hasn't felt the helplessness and grief described in this book, but Aspies in particular *already* struggle with many of the issues the suicide of a loved one brings into their lives. The healing process is hindered, resources to help Aspies are lacking, and the sensory issues are overwhelming.

This book will also be valuable for friends, families, therapists, psychologists, psychiatrists, teachers, and first responders who are or who find themselves in the lives of Aspies and others who have great difficulties with sensory issues, new experiences, and slow processing speeds. It will help those people in understanding what their loved one or friend is going through, and how to help them.

Chapter One
June 24, 2015

Looking back

In hindsight, I wasn't prepared at all for what I'm going to tell you next. You might say, "who is prepared to find the dead, decomposing body of their husband on a normal Wednesday afternoon in June, right before dinner?" No one, but that's not exactly what I'm talking about. I'm referring to the experience as a whole that night, from beginning to end, starting from the phone call and ending with my daughter and I going into the house to face the horror my husband had done to himself and to our family.

I was not prepared to advocate for myself. I was not prepared to tell the police, detective, victim advocate, neighbor, or my family what I needed. I was not prepared for all the bombardment of negative sensory overload, to be battling out-of-control anxiety—while having to listen to important information and answer serious questions. I needed time alone to process, to gather my thoughts together so I could do what needed to be done, but there was no time.

The phone call

It was a regular Wednesday afternoon in June. I'd had an uneventful day working at summer camp. The kids were playing video games and I was just getting ready to make supper when the phone rang. I don't like talking on the phone and didn't know who it was, but I answered it anyway. It ended up being the worst phone call of my life, and the beginning of the end of the life I was building for myself and my two youngest boys, then ages 11 and 12. The person on the other end was Helena, a neighbor, who lived across the street from where my husband still lived in our house about a half hour north of where the boys and I were staying at the time. We had moved out several months before as a separation from my husband, because he was having such a hard time with an undiagnosed mental illness, and the boys and I were safer living elsewhere. Helena told me the police were at my house, and asked if I would like to talk with one of them. I didn't, but did anyway, and the police asked me to bring a key to the house so they could do a wellness check. I said I would and made arrangements to meet them in about a half hour. "Why can't Paul just let them in?" I wondered. "Where is he?"

◇◇◇◇◇◇ Let me explain/It would be so helpful

Talking on the phone is not my favorite way to communicate, because essentially everything I use to analyze whether a conversation is going well or not is unavailable—I can't see the other person's face, small talk is brutal if there's no physical connection with the person I'm talking to, and I never can tell when it's a good time to end a phone call.

Phone calls can easily lead to misunderstandings and miscommunication. I'm slightly more comfortable if I can be honest with the person I'm talking to, even to the point where, when I'm done talking, I can just say that I'm done and end the call. It would be very helpful to be honest when someone calls you, and to let the caller know right away that you prefer other means of communication. I have started requesting emails or texts, if at all possible. These allow time to formulate thoughts, to pick just the right words, and to write exactly what you want to say the way you want to say it.

It would also be very helpful for the caller to be understanding and flexible with someone who doesn't like talking on the phone. It would definitely be helpful if the caller could go with the flow as far as letting the person, who is uncomfortable speaking, lead, and not take offense if it's just the facts and then the call is done.

Another helpful idea for the person who doesn't like talking on the phone could be to let the other speaker know there's only so much time for the call, which would hopefully cause the other speaker to get right to the reason for the phone call, without the extra small talk and pleasantries, which can be for another, less stressful, time.

◇◇◇◇◇◇

The ride to the house

As I anxiously drove north to open the house for the police, all kinds of different scenarios were running through my mind. Had Paul left for Costa Rica and taken all the money, like he said he would? Was he in the house, dead? Had he gone to see a movie and just wasn't home? Why did the police want to get into the house? Had he gone to Las Vegas to gamble and drink all our money and his life away, like he said he would? Was he in the house, dead? Had he taken a little trip somewhere and not told anyone? Was he just at work? Was he dead? I had a sinking feeling my life was about to change and I was helpless to do anything about it, so I just kept driving towards a situation I wanted to get away from as fast as I could in the other direction.

◇◇◇◇◇◇ Let me explain/It would be so helpful

I live with anxiety. It's a constant battle on a good day. During the time I was driving up to the house to give my key to a police officer, I was already feeling like I had lost the battle to control my anxiety, and was so anxious that I had to pay extra attention to driving safely.

Anxiety leads to physical changes. My breathing accelerates and I have to try to concentrate on regulating it. My stomach hurts, my muscles are very tense, and whether there's a reason or not, I have a feeling of impending doom. It's helpful to be able to tell someone that my anxiety is rising so they can talk me back down, which would help get my breathing more regular and alleviate some of the other physical symptoms. It also helps if someone can tell me what's actually happening instead of me relying on my anxious mind to determine the seriousness of the situation.

If you find yourself alone with anxiety rising, the first thing to do to help yourself is to concentrate on your breathing. The goal is to bring your rapid breathing to a more normal level by being conscious of each breath you take. The next thing I do is start talking myself down. I try to not let myself exaggerate a situation. I'm not always successful, but at least I try, which is half the battle right there.

With high levels of anxiety it's very easy to give in to the impending doom part and have a full-blown panic attack, which is not good. It would be so helpful for you to be aware of what's actually happening. Most likely, it's your thoughts causing the anxiety, and not a real crisis or emergency.

◇◇◇◇◇◇

The police

When I arrived at the house there were six police cars lined up in the street by my driveway. All the cars had their bright, blinking lights on, which caused me to be disoriented as they twirled around.

◇◇◇◇◇◇ Let me explain/It would be so helpful

I see everything. I take in the sights, sounds, smells, and feel of an environment, especially in a new, unfamiliar one. The blinking lights of the six police cars drowned out all my other senses and left me disoriented and confused. I didn't think the lights were necessary, and they added a whole new dimension of anxiety to my experience.

Although I am very used to handling anxiety, the energy it took to handle that situation, with the added blinking lights, was physically exhausting, and I still had the whole night to get through.

The police didn't know my reaction to the lights or the effect they had on me, and I was too caught up in trying to orient myself and focus on what I needed to do to tell them what I was struggling with, even if ultimately all the lights had to stay on for some reason.

It would have been better for me if I had had the training to be able to advocate for myself in any situation. Now that I know I would benefit from that kind of training, I can prepare a statement of who I am, what I struggle with, what I need, and any triggers that could bring me to a place of needing nonjudgmental understanding. This training would have to have a component of regular practice with it so it can be done under extreme situations where your memory and coping skills are maxed out.

Advocating can also be in the form of a laminated card made to be given to first responders stating your name, your diagnosis, what the diagnosis manifests into under certain conditions, and the name and number of an understanding family member or friend who can come and help you advocate for yourself. The card could also state what you need—such as a quiet place without flashing lights, loud noises, and lots of people.

◇◇◇◇◇◇

The garage

I tried to open the garage doors with two separate garage door openers, but neither one would work. I knew the police were going to keep me out of the house, and I was disappointed when the garage doors stayed closed.

I reluctantly gave the police my key. They wouldn't let me even go up to the walkway by the front door of the house. They left me standing in the driveway next to the garage while they checked the house. The police told me it was better for me to wait outside to protect me from anything they might find inside.

They left me all alone outside by the garage doors, where, as I stood there, I could smell the decay of my husband's body. I remember thinking it smelled just like a mouse that had gotten stuck in the wall. How ironic that they left me out there alone, near enough to my husband's body to smell the decomposition, to protect me from having the experience of finding something awful inside the house with them.

I'm sure it was protocol and it was thoughtful of them, but the police didn't know my sense of smell was so much keener than the norm, and so for me, as an Aspie, I was traumatized. If I wasn't so filled with anxiety, I possibly could've asked for one of them to stay with me, or I could have stood much farther away from the house.

I also remember I didn't know what to do or where to stand, so I stayed rooted to the spot the police told me to stand in. I wanted them to come out and be with me, but at the same time to stay in the house forever and never come out. I wanted to be back home making supper. I wanted to call Paul and hear him answer his phone. I knew before they came back out that I'd never see my husband alive or hear his voice ever again.

◇◇◇◇◇◇ **Let me explain/It would be so helpful**

Although I enjoy solitude, being left alone by the garage where I could smell the decomposition of my husband's body was not a pleasant way to find out he was dead. It was traumatizing for me to be standing there all alone, figuring that out for myself. My vivid mental pictures were coming up with all kinds of horrible scenes of how he had killed himself just behind the garage doors I was standing right next to.

People without sensory issues may not have been able to smell the decomposition and would have been safe standing there until the police came back. I'm not sure the police could smell the decomposition, but they didn't seem to, and had me stand where I could easily smell it.

This would be a situation where training in assertiveness and advocating for myself would have helped my experience to be less stressful. I had other choices I could've made to make the situation easier for me, including moving away from the garage, but at the time, I was too shocked to focus on making the situation better.

◇◇◇◇◇◇

The news

When the police returned they told me what I already knew, that they had found Paul's body in the garage. They surrounded me to keep me safe and to stop me from going into the house. I instantly found myself in the middle of a tight circle of police I didn't know.

My anxiety continued to rise to an uncomfortable level. They didn't know that surrounding me so quickly without warning at that time would be extremely overwhelming. I sat down right there in the middle of the circle of policemen in the driveway, and put my head down. The police may have thought I was overwhelmed by the awful news instead of being overwhelmed by their circling of me.

They had no idea my brain was just beginning to process the news, and the processing would happen over the days and weeks yet to come. After a few minutes one of the policemen helped me up without asking if he could touch me first, another sensory issue that continued to heighten my anxiety.

Then he led me to the other side of the street with his hand on my shoulder, and that's all I could think about: his hand on my shoulder pressing down seemingly too hard, and how much I didn't want it there. I wanted to scream that I didn't want his hand on my shoulder, but intellectually I knew he thought he was doing something nice, and I was too overwhelmed to say anything.

The police went away thinking they had done their best to take care of and soothe a new widow under the circumstances, and they probably did, for a neurotypical woman. What I needed from them was vastly different. I needed them to be able to understand my extreme sensitivity to smells, touch, noise, and new experiences. I watched some of them go, feeling completely misunderstood, overwhelmed, and confused by their actions alone, never mind what I was really there to comprehend.

◇◇◇◇◇◇ **Let me explain/It would be so helpful**

What happened when the police came outside to tell me the news was, unfortunately for me, another traumatic situation. They probably did this as a regular practice, but when they surrounded me to keep me from going into the house, I felt the fight and flight anxiety to just get out of that circle.

So instead, I withdrew as I sat down in the circle of policemen, and put my head down as a way to try to calm myself, as a way to cope with suddenly being surrounded.

The next thing I knew, my arm was being touched by one of them. He took my arm to get me to stand up without telling me first. It was sudden because the police had to go and wanted me to go across the street, but it really only added to my rising anxiety.

One thing I could've done at that point was to ask for a few more minutes to try to calm myself down.

The policeman who led me across the street, by having his hand on my shoulder, had no idea that he, too, was adding to my experience of heightened anxiety. But at the time, how could he have known? The police don't read minds, and I couldn't formulate the words at that time to tell them.

I accepted the help across the street because I was actually more comfortable with the anxiety I live with on a daily basis, albeit very heightened and uncomfortable at that time, than to speak to the policeman to advocate for myself.

I think it would be very helpful if I had practiced being assertive before all this happened, because I wasn't very good at it. I could've taken assertiveness training to begin to practice being assertive, so when I needed it, I would've been ready.

◇◇◇◇◇◇

The detective

After the policeman led me across the street, he left. I literally turned around, and with no time to gather myself together, a detective drove up, introduced himself, and asked me a bunch of questions that started making me feel guilty.

He was just doing his job, I guess he had to find out if I had any part in Paul's death, but at the time I was thinking of so many other things I can't remember much of what he said. I believe the way I was acting while answering his questions could very easily have led the detective to think I was hiding something about Paul's death. It was difficult, with my receptive and expressive language deficits along with high anxiety, to take in his questions and then to formulate coherent answers in a timely manner, so it could have looked like I needed the time to make up some lies.

I couldn't look him in the eye, no matter how much I tried; I was just too overloaded with everything that was happening. But not looking at someone in the eye to a neurotypical person can be another indicator of lying.

Therefore, intellectually I knew how I was probably being perceived by the detective, but I couldn't even begin to explain about Asperger's syndrome—even the thought of it was too exhausting.

◇◇◇◇◇◇ Let me explain/It would be so helpful

When the detective started asking me questions about the situation between Paul and me, I felt like I wasn't presenting myself well at all. I knew I needed to make eye contact because looking away when answering questions can be an indication of lying.

I couldn't make eye contact with the detective, especially when I was thinking about an answer to a question he had asked. I tried hard to keep eye contact or even to look at his forehead or chin, but I couldn't even do that. And to add a long response time to his questions because I was processing slowly at that time could've added to the suspicion that I was lying.

This is important to resolve because I could've become a person of interest due to the way I was acting, although it was caused by sensory issues, having Asperger's, and the trauma of finding Paul in the garage. It would have been helpful to be able to have that short, rehearsed explanation of why I was acting the way I was to help the detective understand my behavior.

It would need to be rehearsed and memorized because when anxiety levels get very high, it's difficult to think clearly and remember what to say. And if your words are all jumbled up in your thoughts and it's difficult to express yourself, again, you might want to have a laminated card to give important information about yourself to the first responder.

◇◇◇◇◇◇

Telling my kids

I had to go into my neighbor's house to tell my boys why there were so many police cars outside our house. I told them the truth, and sat with them while they experienced the first feelings of emptiness and grief that would stay with them in some way, shape, or form for the rest of their lives. It was heart-breaking for me and I was barely holding myself together. Yet this new unfamiliar, scary life was just beginning, and there was nothing I could do about it.

I had called my adult daughter before I told the boys. She headed straight for the house. When she got there, about a half hour later, I was able to ground myself enough to make it through the rest of the night. I was able to do this because she understood me. She knew when to step in and help answer questions while I took a moment to breathe. She validated my feelings because she was experiencing many of the same ones.

I had called my oldest son right after I called my daughter, and talking to him on the phone was also grounding for me. He was so matter-of-fact and detail-oriented that it was refreshing to talk to someone without emotions getting in the way. My phone call with him cleared my head enough to be able to get through what I needed to do that night as well.

◇◇◇◇◇◇ Let me explain/It would be so helpful

Explaining to my two youngest kids what had happened that night reminded me of taking them to get the surgeries they both needed when they were small. I had to tell them because they were going to find out anyway, but at the same time, I knew they were going to be very upset, and it was going to cause them pain. It hurt me to tell them.

If I could've shielded them from ever knowing I would have done it. The boy's reactions were emotional, but after a while I encouraged them to try to play with their friend while they stayed at his house for a few hours. I checked on them once in a while, and although they were sad, they were doing okay. I'm not sure they understood the finality of what happened until some time went by and they were able to process the information. Telling them was another terrible part of an awful experience.

My two adult children were very helpful to my state of being. They helped me to calm down a bit and get through the rest of the night. My daughter lived close by and was at the house with me until it was over for the night. She understood me and it was such a relief to be understood, not to have to explain myself, and have someone there to experience the death of a loved one together.

My son lives about 1400 miles away and was still a big help to me because I could relate to him comfortably, and again, I didn't have to explain myself. My kids were and continue to be a lifeline for me, all in their own way.

It would be helpful to contact family or friends who know and understand you so you can relax and be yourself with someone during the extremely emotional, confusing, painful experience of losing someone you love by suicide. If they are too far away to come and be with you, talking to them on the phone or texting them can also help you feel like you're not alone.

◇◇◇◇◇◇

The victim advocate

The victim advocate showed up with a dog, right around the same time as I was talking to the detective. Her therapy dog was too much extra stimulus for me at the time, and so he did not serve the purpose he was there for; in fact, it was just the opposite. The kind victim advocate and her therapy dog were only adding to the overwhelming sensory overload and anxiety that I had been fighting a losing battle over all night.

I remember she kept asking me to sit in her car because there were bugs outside once the sun went down, which was a thoughtful gesture. I just couldn't sit. I had to walk around while getting my anxiety and sensory overload back in control. She kept asking and asking if I wanted to sit in her car. Again, she was being thoughtful, yet every time she asked, my anxiety went up.

Finally my daughter asked her if she, herself, wanted to sit in her car; I believe the victim advocate said yes and went and sat in her car for a while. The victim advocate also asked me several times how the boys were doing. Now I don't know how I would've reacted to those questions in a regular, sane situation, but that night, as I was standing across the street from where my husband had died, all I saw were implications.

How was I supposed to know how the boys were doing? Right or wrong, I got very irritated with that question. Like I said, I felt there were implications embedded in that question, such as: was I forgetting the boys, or why wasn't I with them? I knew my reasons. My boys were playing with their friend at a neighbor's house, they didn't want to come outside, I didn't want them outside, they were going to be fed supper there, and were much better off where they were than outside, with me.

Unfortunately, the victim advocate added to my anxiety and the negative aspect of the whole experience. I found that to be true in the weeks to come as well. I don't think she ever really helped me with anything, although she seemed to have tried.

She offered to help me get the police report, to put me in contact with the right people to get Paul's personal property back, and to find the right detective because the detectives in charge of the case changed a couple of times.

Those offers would have been very helpful to me, but none of them actually happened. I had to find all those things myself. She was a busy lady. I had to spend a lot of time on the phone trying to reach her. I'm not saying this to put blame on her as a person, but more to explain my reaction to her job.

◇◇◇◇◇◇ Let me explain/It would be so helpful

Okay, I'm all for having a victim advocate on the scene to help someone who can truly benefit from them being there to help. But with my anxiety as high as it was, and with my senses all haywire, the victim advocate was not helpful to me.

She stood too near, talked too much, let her dog get really close, gave me too much information, and I felt she misunderstood how I was choosing to care for my youngest two boys. I'm sure she is very helpful to some people who need the closeness of someone, anyone, even a complete stranger like a victim advocate, at the time of a crisis.

What would have been helpful was for her to let me know she was there, and then let me lead any conversation, information gathering, dog hugging, or implications. If she had let me go to her, I would have been much more comfortable with her being there for me. It would be helpful for victim advocates to be able to work with all people, even people on the spectrum, and not think that everyone needs the same kind of connection or attention.

One way that the victim advocate could've helped me was to introduce herself, tell me she was there, give me a quick synopsis of what she could do as a victim advocate, ask me if I needed anything, and then stand aside until I needed her.

The most pertinent, valuable, supportive way she helped me was to give me pamphlets of information. Giving me those pamphlets required no talking, no closeness, no questions, and all I needed to know was right there at my fingertips to look at when I was much less stressed.

Again, I could've used a short, rehearsed explanation to tell her what I needed from her. I would encourage everyone to be prepared to have to advocate for themselves at a moment's notice and in any possible anxiety-filled, emotional state.

It will be very useful to be prepared to help yourself in case something as devastating as the suicide of a loved one happens unexpectedly. This could include a short, well-rehearsed explanation of your diagnosis, struggles, and needs. The information can be on a laminated card to just show the people you need to communicate with at that time.

◇◇◇◇◇◇

Reality

I had to see Paul's body come out of the house. For my own peace of mind, and to be able to cement the reality in my head, I had to see his body being brought out and put into the coroner's van.

The medical examiner would not remove the body with me watching. She wanted to protect me. I really wish she had just asked me what I wanted. I could've had a conversation with her about what I needed. She didn't understand my visual thinking would make it much worse a scenario than reality, so I knew I needed to see the reality to rely on whenever I thought of this night in the future.

This time I would not be swayed and I did make my needs known. I knew the experience I could have with my own visual thinking would be so much worse than to actually see Paul's body come out of the garage and be put into the van.

Finally there was a compromise, and I could watch from across the street. Even with the compromise, the medical examiner positioned the van so that I could see very little. I did manage to see his body being brought out on a gurney. I had to keep repeating to myself that it was really his body. It was very bloated from the state of decomposition it was in, which is why his body looked so big, but at least I was able to see it actually being brought out of the house and put into the truck.

That's when I cried for the first time that night.

◇◇◇◇◇◇ Let me explain/It would be so helpful

I am a visual thinker. When a memory comes to mind, I can see it as a still picture or a video; if I'm trying to remember a word, I see it written down; or I remember a number by reading it off a piece of paper in my mind.

I knew I had to see Paul's body come out of the garage so I could have something to visualize in my mind that was real, instead of letting my imagination go wild and visualize a more graphic, ugly scene. The medical examiner didn't understand. There was a certain protocol put into place for every crime scene they went to where there was a body to take away. The loved one was to be somewhere else and not shown any of the process of removing the body.

I'm sure this works for most people, but I needed something different. I needed to see my husband's body leave the house. The medical examiner was not going to change anything to meet my needs. I did advocate for myself in this part of my experience because I knew I would have such a difficult time if I didn't see the body leave the house. We were able to come to a compromise, but it was me who got the short end of the stick and the medical examiner who got to do things mostly her way. This was another area where it would've been helpful if I had been more assertive. I did not have any training in being assertive at that time.

I thought it would've been very helpful if the medical examiner was more conscious of the needs of different people, but that really wouldn't work out because no one is the same, and standard protocol is needed in an emotionally charged situation.

The next very helpful skill would have been to be able to recognize the situation for what it was, see the limitations that came with it, and to try to be flexible. There's one thing I've learned since I've been on this journey, and it's that as much as we'd like the world to accept and embrace us in our different ways of thinking and being, we must also work just as hard to accept and embrace the world even with our unique ways of interacting, such as with rigidness, black and white thinking, sensory issues, and awkward social skills.

Chapter Two

The Aftermath Begins

The smell

Once the two policemen who had stayed to help the medical examiner take Paul's body out of the garage were finished, they returned my key, told me the house was mine again, and then they left.

My daughter and I tentatively went into the house to face the horror of what my husband had done to himself. The smell of decomposition was everywhere in the house, especially the garage. I am sensitive to smells, and had a very difficult time being in the house, yet I couldn't stay away. We searched for a clue, a reason for why he had completed suicide. We couldn't find anything, but it helped a bit just to look. It was difficult for me to be at the house.

The first time I went into the garage it seemed surreal, especially with the smell. I knew they had taken Paul's body out of his car and laid him on the floor because I saw the motions of doing that from across the street. Plus I had heard a shout to an officer to help them pull Paul out of the car. They must have laid him on a sheet because there were two new stains on the garage floor, which was probably where Paul's head and feet overlapped the sheet.

I would go look at those two places in the garage that were stained by Paul's body as they were wrapping it up and getting it onto the gurney to take it away. One was at his head and one was six feet away, at his feet. It was all I had left of him, and although people kept telling me not to go in there and look, it helped me to process his death. I needed the visual, and although what I saw in the car and on the floor of the garage was not pleasant, it was more pleasant than what my own very visual thinking brain could conjure up.

As my daughter and I searched for some meaning to this new twist in our lives, both of us kept going into the garage from the house. I felt like I was closer to him out there, and thought maybe I could find something, one thing that would make sense. I never found it. Nothing made sense.

The next day, when we got to the house, we had to do something with Paul's car. I called his insurance agency and at first the insurance agent said I couldn't request to tow the car away because it wasn't in my name.

I reminded her that the owner's body had decomposed for several days in that car, inside a closed garage, in the hot, humid, Florida weather, but she wouldn't change her mind. As far as she was concerned, the car was staying at my house and that was that.

So I was freaking out when the car appraiser came to assess the damage. I needed that car to be gone. He walked into the garage, immediately walked back out, and told me he was having the car towed that day. I told him what the lady on the phone had said, and he just repeated that the car would be towed that day. It was actually towed within an hour.

We had to clean out Paul's belongings from the car before it was towed away. My daughter cleaned out the front passenger seat, which was closer to where he actually was when he died, and I cleaned out the back seat. The car contained residual indications of his death both visually and by smell, which, as unpleasant as that was, also helped both of us to continue to process that he was really gone. When the appraiser came to say goodbye to me, he had a tear running down his cheek, or he was sweating, but I think it was a tear. He was one of the good guys.

◇◇◇◇◇◇ Let me explain/It would be so helpful

There are images seared into my memory. Like pictures on a camera, they are all stored and will come out when I'm reminded of them. The smell left in the house and garage was seared into my memory like the images. I couldn't un-smell it. I couldn't forget about it. The smell relentlessly haunted me for the first few months after Paul's death.

With the smell came all the feelings I felt that first night. If I had made any progress forward in my grief work, the smell threw me back enough to feel like it had all been wiped away. It came back if any other smell reminded me even just a little bit of the smell in the house and garage.

I could be just fine, walk by a sink with dirty dishes in it or a trash can that needed emptying and be transported immediately back to the night we found Paul's body. The sudden sensory slam would unnerve me and leave me feeling like I would never be able to get away from the damage that smell was causing to my well-being.

There were days the smell would be with me all day. There were also days the smell would come, flood me with the feelings of that night, and leave as quickly as it came, although the feelings would linger. It would've been helpful if I could have somehow managed to come to peace with the smell and what it represented. What I did do was to put certain pleasant smells under my nose. To be honest, it helped sometimes, but not all the time. It is something to try to see if it is helpful.

I found that writing about it helped a great deal too. Drawing helped to sort out some of the feelings the smell brought back to me as well. While it hurt emotionally during the time I was writing and drawing, I always felt better afterwards. Listening to music is another way I helped myself to get through all the feelings that smell would bring of the night we found Paul.

One other helpful skill was to talk to someone about how I was feeling. Yes, skill, because with any social interaction I had to use the social skills I've learned throughout the years. Although I have never understood it, I have experienced the relief and lightness that comes after telling someone how I feel. I couldn't just tell anyone; it had to be someone who understood and listened to what I was saying with no judgment.

The way to discern the people who will listen is that they have listened before. They have listened even if what you were saying at a different time and place was benign small talk, like what you were doing that weekend. If they truly listened and heard you, that would be one person you could talk to about how you were feeling.

Remember, you still have to discern if they are ready to listen to the heavy stuff of what might be on your mind. There is an easy way to find that out—ask them. Ask them if it's okay if you talk to them about the heavier stuff having to do with a completed suicide. You can give them permission to say no, or at least tell them you'd appreciate their honesty. It would be a mistake if someone said yes because they didn't want to be rude, or hurt your feelings, or leave you with no one to talk to.

I have found that neurotypical people will tell a little white lie if they believe the truth will hurt you. You have to convince them that you really, truly want the truth, and that it would be worse to have someone not be honest with you. They might not get it at first, but if you keep reassuring them, they will eventually believe you and reward you with their honesty.

I came to know whom I could talk to about different things. There were people who wanted to talk and help, but I could only talk to them about ordinary day-to-day activities. There were other people I could talk to about some heavier, more serious issues, and lastly, there were a couple of people I could talk to about anything.

◇◇◇◇◇◇

The first week

The week right after Paul completed suicide we had family come to stay with us. Our son Ben and Paul's father, step-mother, and sister traveled down south to be with me, Rachel, and the boys. My friend Carla and her family cut their vacation short so Carla could be there for me and my family. There were people who couldn't make the trip down south who still let us know they were thinking about us from where they were. There were a couple of times I felt overwhelmed with everything, and during those times I would get busy doing something only I could do to give myself a small break.

◇◇◇◇◇◇ Let me explain/It would be so helpful

I can't remember everything about the first week, but I do remember who came to be with me and my family. I was glad they were there. It gave me something else to think about for a while. I wasn't overwhelmed by their visit because only three of Paul's family came down. Others sent cards, called, or sent well-wishes through other people. I had to be strong while they were visiting, and I was able to put off feeling too much grief until after they left and I was alone.

If you have people who could stay with you for a while and it helps to have them there, then by all means, welcome them and enjoy their company the best you can after experiencing the death of a loved one to suicide.

But if you are overwhelmed by having people over to see you, make your needs known. You could tell them that you appreciate their willingness to be with you to keep you company, but you need time alone. If a friend or loved one doesn't have the energy or desire for company, the best thing to do is honor their request, but you can still keep in touch through quick phone calls, texts, emails, or a card in the mail.

If you start to feel overwhelmed while people are there with you to give you companionship and company, you could excuse yourself and take a nap, take a walk, start cleaning for guests, or prepare something to eat for everyone. And if it helps, listen to music while you nap, walk, or work.

◇◇◇◇◇◇

The clean-up

The first task was to get the house ready to sell. Unfortunately, the smell in the house became the center of a dispute between the insurance company and the bio-hazard cleaning company. I had people from the insurance company come into my home and say they smelled nothing out of the ordinary. This was while I was almost gagging over the smell and had sinus pain and a headache.

Then the bio-hazard people would come to the house and say the smell was overwhelming. I kept asking for science—science to objectively measure the levels of carbon monoxide, or body decomposition chemicals, or whatever was in the house.

Finally the insurance company agreed, and they hired a consultant to measure the levels of chemicals in the air. The results were conclusive that there were hazardous levels of certain chemicals in the air in my home due to the decomposition of my husband's body.

The bio-hazard clean-up crew finally started working on cleaning my house about six weeks after Paul died. I wholeheartedly believe that if I'd had the skills to be assertive when needed, state clearly what I wanted done, and to follow through with what I was asking for, it would not have taken six weeks to begin the cleaning of the bio-waste products from my home.

◇◇◇◇◇◇ **Let me explain/It would be so helpful**

As I dealt with the bio-hazard cleaning company I was very careful about trying to understand and make the right decisions. I was careful for each different social business situation that came up in dealing with the aftermath of Paul's suicide. I'm very black and white in my thinking, and that kept leading to misunderstandings with people I had to interact with about settling Paul's estate.

The people I talked to would either exaggerate a situation that I took literally, or downplay a situation that I also took literally. I never knew what to expect, and had to be diligent in determining if I was being taken advantage of or not. It's helpful to have someone you trust to discuss these social business situations with, to make sure people are being fair and honest with you.

The hardest one for me was the bio-hazard clean-up crew I hired to restore my house to the way it was before Paul completed suicide. There were so many times I was told one thing only to have the bio-hazard company do something else. I never knew what was going to happen until it actually happened. The deadlines were never met, the work was never done as it was explained to me, and I heard a different story about the restoration of my home every time I talked with the owner of the company. I felt helplessness in trying to get my house clean enough for it to be safe to sell. It ended up needing to be completely repainted, and what I was told would be a four-day job turned into a four-week job.

The house was not ready to put on the market until October, and Paul had died in June. Meanwhile I was paying the mortgage every month for a place I didn't live in, didn't want anymore, and couldn't really afford. It would've been very helpful to have someone right there with me who could've helped me interpret what was being said to me about my home as opposed to what was actually being done to my home. I needed someone who could've validated how I felt about the bio-hazard company and helped me to advocate for myself.

If you have no such person in your life, you could try to work out better communication with the owner of the company and ask for everything to be put into writing so you could read it and re-read it to make sense out of what was being said and done. You could also ask another bio-hazard company how long it takes them, the cost, access to your home, and a myriad of other questions that can and will need to be understood, so you can compare that information to the information you're being given from the bio-hazard company you hired.

In hindsight, I do wish I had gotten everything in writing, including dates and times of when the work would be done such as overall deadlines of work completion. I must, though, give myself some credit for the things I did right during the process of cleaning my home. First, I listened to my two adult children who both had so much knowledge about the science and business behind the clean-up and contract with the bio-hazard company that they really helped me to be a wise consumer.

I also got one piece of the contract changed to reflect what I was being told in person, which contradicted what was written in the contract, and I got that change signed by the owner of the company, and then showed my lawyer the signature so he could tell me if it was contractually binding or not. I was relieved to know it was good enough to be held up in court if needed.

I asked a male friend to join me on a conference call when I talked to the owner who was continuously frustrated with me. I'm still not sure exactly what he was frustrated about; I was only holding him to what he said he would do, but having my friend on the line helped tremendously. The owner was suddenly calm, helpful, and willing to compromise with me so we could come up with a solution that worked for both of us.

Please don't hesitate to ask a friend to interpret a situation that is difficult to figure out. No matter how old you are, there's no shame in asking for help. Everyone has areas of strengths and weaknesses. I personally feel it's courageous to know your strengths and accept (yet continue to work on) your weaknesses to the point where you realize at times you need help.

It takes courage and humility to ask for help knowing that most other adults don't even have to think about doing what is very challenging to some people on the spectrum. Yet there are other areas where people on the spectrum excel, so it all comes out in the wash—although I have no idea what any of this has to do with water, detergent, and clothes.

◇◇◇◇◇◇

More phone calls

As I was dealing with the bio-hazard cleaning company I also had to make many phone calls to other places of business to handle my husband's affairs. I felt like a full-time secretary who hates paperwork and doesn't like to talk on the phone, but no matter how badly I messed up, there was no one to fire me, which would have been appreciated.

The phone calls were the worst of my secretarial tasks because I can't see the face of the person I'm talking to, and that unnerves me and makes me feel like I have too much of a chance to misinterpret the conversation. I never know when to say goodbye, and am often stuck on the phone long after I want to hang up.

Paul and I used to talk on the phone a lot while he was traveling for his job. We had a system where if one of us was done talking, we just told the other that, "I have nothing else to say to you." It was not said in anger or sarcasm or anything negative, in fact, it was just the opposite. It showed we were able to be open and honest with each other, and was a positive indication of how close of a relationship we had together at that time.

After Paul's death there were days when I was on the phone all day long. Literally all day long, with short breaks, and did not accomplish anything! So I was on the phone the next day too. I can't even begin to calculate how many hours I sat there on hold, only to be transferred to another person, who transferred me to another person, who was busy, so I left a message that was never returned.

One of my frustrations was making sure everything was understood before I hung up, only to call back and get a different person so I had to start all over again, or get the same person and have them not know anything we had previously talked about.

The people on the other end of the phone would express their sympathy by saying they were sorry for my loss. After a while I came to resent them saying that because it became rote; maybe it was the politically correct thing to say, or it may have been protocol they'd been given to say in a case where someone had died. I have never liked platitudes.

But alas, this was probably just one of those things people say that make no sense to me and that I believe most of them don't really mean. I could tell who had sincerity in their voice and possibly cared out of a genuine love for humanity. Those calls were at least okay.

There were a couple of phone calls when even though I had sent a death certificate in to prove he had died and I had previously talked with them several times, they would still not give me information because they needed to speak to the main account holder, Paul.

So in frustration, one day I told someone where they could find him. I explained they could look in one of two places and perhaps they would run into him. They could go to the Pearly Gates and ask St Peter if he'd seen Paul and if so, could he get a message to him about his account… or, if St Peter hadn't seen him, to get ready to be really, really hot! Surprisingly, the person on the other end of the phone did not understand my words this time, and for some strange reason, that helped me feel a little bit better.

◇◇◇◇◇◇ Let me explain/It would be so helpful

I dreaded the phone calls I had to make to take care of Paul's affairs. While I spent the majority of time on hold after talking to a machine, when I did finally get to talk to a person, I knew I'd either have someone who was kind and understanding or who was grouchy and uncaring. It was so emotionally exhausting. It was like making small talk all day long to several different people.

Some people did understand how difficult certain phone calls were because of what I was calling about, and others were impatient with me for one reason or another. I would have to call back to the same place several times over about the same situation and get a different person each time, which meant I'd have to start all over again from scratch, just like it was the very first call. I tried everything I could think of to help the person I was calling to understand the reason for the phone call, but alas, I'd find myself having to explain it all over again from scratch every time I called anyway.

I always try to say what I mean and mean what I say. I'm very careful to choose the right words to say when I'm talking to someone. I only let myself relax from this strict rule I've set for myself if I'm with people I'm very comfortable with, and even then I'm cautious.

The reason I'm so careful is the many times that I've said the wrong thing and all of a sudden someone is angry with me and I have no idea why. I usually find that it's because I had mistakenly said something rude to whomever I was talking to and they took offense at it.

On the other hand, I sometimes have trouble understanding what other people say to me, such as when strangers would say they were "sorry" Paul died. I can understand close friends and family saying that because they probably are truly sorry that he died and I'm hurt from the loss. I have never understood strangers saying "I'm sorry for your loss" to me when they don't know me, unless they are saying it in general, from one human being to another.

I've thought a lot about it and I think what I would say if someone told me they just lost a loved one is, "That must be difficult for you. Is there any way I can help?" All of these chances of misunderstanding and miscommunication are more likely to happen while talking on the phone.

When using the phone to communicate there's no way of telling how the other person is feeling. All you can go by is their voice, and it's difficult to discern emotions just by using a voice. There are times it's obvious that someone is sad, happy, or angry, but there's really no way at all to tell if someone is bored, getting frustrated, or experiencing other subtle emotions.

Talking on the phone is difficult on a good day and is near impossible when you are already overwhelmed as a survivor of suicide loss. It would be helpful to communicate by text or in person if that works, but if you can only communicate by phone, you can help the situation by letting the person you are calling know right away that you are uncomfortable communicating this way, and then state what you need clearly, stick with the facts, and end the phone call as soon as your business is finished.

I would also suggest being proactive. If you know you do not like talking on the phone, practice talking on the phone. You will be doing yourself a favor by practicing before you are in a situation where there is no choice about whether you communicate by phone or not. It may be out of your comfort zone, but that's okay. Stretching yourself to experience new ways to communicate will help you right away in your everyday life, not just when you have an emergency.

◇◇◇◇◇◇

Business

I had so many people I needed to talk to it was exhausting. I had to talk to people at Paul's work to finalize his employment status. I had to talk to his doctors, insurance companies, my lawyer, the mortgage company, the bio-hazard cleaning crew, and the police as I tried to get his personal property returned.

One thing I struggled with was my slow processing speed. I'd have a conversation with someone and not fully process the conversation until a few hours or even a day later. But that didn't stop people from needing to talk with me, so I'd have even more conversations to process.

I'd have a conversation where we may have talked about a certain decision I needed to make, but the time it took for me to process that conversation could be up to a day long. That meant that most of the time I was just going through the motions until I was able to process the conversation to the point where I could put what was discussed into action.

One of the problems with that is I could never remember the last thing I had done, or even what I had done right after I did it. I started writing everything down in a journal, and that helped a lot. There were so many times that I looked back in my book and was very surprised to see that I had already done something I thought I still needed to do.

It was common to have a day where I spent time on the phone talking to several business places, and was inundated with times, days, information, and not able to remember much about any of the calls.

One day I called the police station and victim advocate to once again begin the process of reclaiming Paul's property, and the coroner's office to try to get information on the cause of death. The people at the police station and the victim advocate were difficult to get a hold of, but they would return phone calls after a day or two. Eventually I had to just go to the police station in person to get done what I had to do.

◇◇◇◇◇◇ Let me explain/It would be so helpful

In the weeks after the night my husband was found, I was struggling with all the information coming in from several directions, such as figuring out the finances, making insurance claims, talking to the human resources people from my husband's workplace as they wrapped up the little details of his employment, etc.

My friend Carla suggested I make a binder to keep track of everything. Although I thought it was a great idea, to be honest I couldn't go to the store, buy one, make the tabs, and then organize my notes and paperwork, even though it would've helped me immensely. I didn't have the motivation to bring that idea to fruition.

I was pleasantly surprised and also very relieved when she made one for me. It quickly became a valuable tool. I'm not a naturally organized person. I dislike anything to do with business, accounts, finances, bill paying, and phone calls, all of which I had to work out day after day after day.

I'm still not completely finished settling his affairs and getting everything in my name. I'm not proficient in handling my finances in the best way yet. I'm still learning and making the best decisions I can with what I know at any given moment. Despite my struggles, I kept trying, and one thing I did for myself was start filing my paperwork in the binder and found that it did work quite well at organizing paperwork.

After several times of finding what I needed quickly because it was filed away correctly, I was sold on the binder and started to really rely on it. I made myself file paperwork away immediately after getting new documents, working with old documents, paying bills, and dealing with Paul's accounts.

I didn't have to worry so much anymore about remembering everything. I could trust myself enough to only have to remember what categories in the binder all the different paperwork was filed under so I could easily find any information I needed. I kept up with writing down information in my journal when I made calls, what the calls were about, what was accomplished, if I had to return any calls, and who was going to be returning phone calls to me. I started feeling more and more that I could handle the affairs that needed to be cleaned up and settled from my husband's death.

Although that positive feeling of being able to handle the affairs would come and go for a while, the binder was always there, providing me with the information I needed when I couldn't remember on my own. It would be so helpful to an overwhelmed, grief-stricken, anxiety-filled person to have a system to organize all the information swirling around in their head.

◇◇◇◇◇◇

Decisions

While I was making progress in organizing the information I had to keep track of, there was one part of settling Paul's affairs that I couldn't fix with a binder or journal. What I'm referring to was the part where I hadn't made an important decision in years. My husband was the decision-maker in our family and for my life. I could give my advice, although it was usually taken with a grain of salt, dismissed, and he would make the decision on his own.

Although I know in my heart that some of my dismissed decisions were ultimately the right ones, I really have never known if they would've turned out like I thought they would because they were never tried.

I was now on my own to make all the decisions in the family, although my days were full of anxiety, grief, frustration, and confusion. I repeatedly had to accomplish new tasks, sometimes in moment-by-moment increments, with my faculties in desperate disarray. I couldn't think, I couldn't speak, or process information coming in, and it seemed like I couldn't remember anything. In spite of my mental and emotional state, I still had to make critically important life decisions. Making decisions was a new and unfamiliar task I took on at a time I was preforming at my worst.

One of the places I had to make decisions soon after Paul's death was at the crematorium. There was a woman there who was all business and facts, and a woman who was emotional and reassuring. I was so very glad to have the woman who was all business and facts to talk to and make arrangements with. I could not have worked with Ms. Emotion, as kind as she was, because my emotions would have been all over the place. Interacting with Ms. Facts allowed me to keep my composure, and to be able to process the information she was presenting to me and manage to calm my thoughts enough to think before I made the decisions about Paul's cremation.

As I meandered through the next few months I was forced to make important life decisions, mostly with finances, which was part of the responsibilities of my new life that I understood the least.

As I took a real-life crash course in decision-making, I made both wise and stupid decisions. I learned in a trial-by-fire way to make decisions quickly as I went along. I should've been experienced at this by my age, but I wasn't because I had never had a chance to practice. Paul had made all the decisions in our family. One positive aspect of being in this predicament was the more decisions I made, the stronger I felt. I started entertaining the thought of actually making it on my own. I felt more confident, even with some of the bad decisions I made, because I understood it was a learning experience.

◇◇◇◇◇◇ Let me explain/It would be so helpful

Part of the new normal for me was to make decisions. I hadn't had the practice of making important decisions the whole time I was married, which, at the time of Paul's death, was 29 years. I also had to make decisions about things that I didn't understand, like finances, and these decisions were important for the present and the future well-being of my family. I felt very inadequate, and rightfully so, because I was also doing all this while filled with anxiety, grief, and sensory issues that hindered my already poor decision-making skills. I had to learn and learn fast.

Unfortunately, I can't remember information I'm not interested in, so I was reading and re-reading financial information over and over again. What I found helpful was to take notes. Writing information down always helps me to remember it because I can see what I wrote in my mind if I need to refer back to it. I also had the notes to take with me to meetings with bankers and financial advisors.

I learned to make good use of any resources available. There are online tutorials, banks have employees to help explain things to you, and there's always someone who has done the finances in their family for years who can help if you ask them.

My mother, Grace, was the one who helped me the most in the area of finances. She has been in charge of the finances in our family for over 55 years, and has learned a lot during that time. She also put me in contact with her financial advisor, who helped me as a middle man on my side while I worked with the company holding the assets of which I was the beneficiary.

I tried to work with a company of financial advisors and planners affiliated with my bank, but I got nervous with all the plans for my money they were talking about together, as if I wasn't there, and I stopped working with them. So even when I was not proficient in money matters, I still trusted my instincts and walked away when conversations didn't feel right. Sometimes there are matters where the only one you have to trust is yourself.

◇◇◇◇◇◇

Self-preservation

One day, soon after we found Paul, I was having a difficult time with everything that needed to be done. I was emotional and overwhelmed as I tried to finish all the business that needed to be done. One of my errands was to go to the crematorium and make arrangements for the cremation, the place where I was very glad to have been helped by Ms. Facts instead of Ms. Emotions as I made my decisions. What I'm talking about here is when I left the crematorium and I was still in the parking lot, composing myself enough to drive.

My friend Carla, who was doing everything she could to help me, and the bio-hazard guy I was hiring to work on my house, drove up next to me. He started telling me all he was going to do for me in such detail and in so many words that I might as well have been underwater trying to listen to him. At this point, to say that I was overwhelmed or on sensory overload just doesn't even begin to describe my mental and emotional state.

I started signing things just on the word of my friend, who I trusted, because this was an area that needed immediate attention. I'm glad she was there. The problem was that I felt like I couldn't take in even one more piece of information, make one more decision, or make any more plans at that point. I had gone into a self-preservation state of mind, and was simply going through the motions while making those very important life decisions.

It was not the ideal situation for me or for anyone to be in. I should have been at home with my boys or resting because I was in no shape mentally, emotionally, or physically to even make the decision of what to have for supper.

◇◇◇◇◇◇ Let me explain/It would be so helpful

Unfortunately, there are matters to be addressed immediately after a loved one completes suicide. These are the most difficult to deal with because of all the emotions of shock, grief, confusion, and sometimes trauma that may have come with the suicide.

Right now, honestly, I can't even remember some days at the very beginning of this journey. The only things I have to remember those days by are any journal entries I wrote, and my writing didn't begin for a couple of weeks after Paul was found. At this time friends and family are needed to help meander back through those days that now are mysterious to me because my recollection of what happened is not clear.

It would be helpful to make use of the local resources available such as the local victim advocate, suicide support groups, and local chapters of national organizations for the prevention of suicide as well as support for survivors of suicide loss.

Although my experience with the victim advocate could have benefited by better communication from both of us, I'm sure the victim advocate can share valuable information with many others who need help. Perhaps using the short, rehearsed explanation of your diagnosis and particular way of communicating will help create a more open, helpful dialogue, enabling the victim advocate to help where needed.

While the situation can't be changed, there are ways to make the best of it by making your needs known to whoever can help. This is one time in your life where help is important, and asking for help is the best way to get assistance for yourself through those first few days, weeks, and even months.

Chapter Three
Where Did Everyone Go?

Loose connections

Connections to other people were another part of my life I struggled with in the aftermath of Paul completing suicide. Along with the difficulties of finances, decision-making, and phone calls, I felt disconnected and awkward with many of the friendships that were comfortable before Paul's death.

My desire is to feel connected to other people; my default state is to feel disconnected to people. Except for family members and friends I consider family, I have difficulty feeling a consistent emotional connection to people. The feeling of being disconnected was exacerbated during the time after Paul's death.

I can usually feel a better connection if the person and I are able spend time together regularly. I can have a friendship and not feel a connection or only feel it at certain times, mostly when we are doing something together face to face, but then, when we are away from each other, the connection can drop out and be gone for me.

Intellectually I know there's still a connection, but emotionally I can't feel it. Since I have always craved a connection to people, I work very hard at trying to do the right thing in a friendship. I try my best, thinking that it will lead me to a relationship where I feel that connection solidly, as I believe I see other people experience.

One example from my own life is having friends who truly care about me, yet no matter how hard I try, and as loyal as they are to the friendship, the emotional connection still waxes and wanes for me. I have to depend on my intellect to muddle out that we are still connected because of the times I don't feel it emotionally.

I had a connection to Paul, but the connection weakened over time as he got sicker and sicker, and now it is gone with him.

I'm happy to say I have never questioned the connection to any of my children. I can feel it strongly and it never wavers. So I know connections can happen. Besides my children, the person I've felt most connected to in my life was my husband, until his illness cruelly stole that from both of us.

◇◇◇◇◇◇ Let me explain/It would be so helpful

If I could have felt more of a connection to the people around me, I know the days, weeks, and months after Paul completed suicide would've been a more comfortable, less lonely period of recovery.

The people near me would offer help, but some were honestly too busy with their own lives to actually follow through, which I can understand. It would have been helpful if I could have understood at the time why they offered help if they knew they already had an extremely busy schedule.

As time went by I did understand that those people were telling me what they wanted to happen, but probably already knew wouldn't. At first, I took their offer to help seriously, and was disappointed and felt rejected and alone when it didn't actually happen.

I had to learn to take what people said with a grain of salt and be thankful for the people who came through with the help they offered, because I believe all the offers truly came from a place of caring. I did have a friend, Alison, who came to visit with me once in a while for companionship, to help with something around the house, or even to get me to go out and have fun.

Even so, most of the time I was home alone struggling with my own thoughts, which wasn't the best way to be spending my days considering my thoughts were definitely not helpful then. The thoughts were unwanted, even though in processing them and trying to make sense of them I had to experience grief and pain, which in a way was healing.

In hindsight, if I wasn't so overwhelmed and thought I needed someone else to tell me how to feel better, I wouldn't have stayed alone so much. I would've asked people to come over or meet for coffee instead of waiting for them to call me to do something together. On the days I needed time alone, I could've had those days too.

It would be helpful if I had come to realize I was the person in charge of my own healing much sooner than I actually did. I was so overwhelmed with everything; I wanted someone to show me the way out of my grief, anxiety, and depression. Only that's not the way it works—friends can give information, encouragement, and companionship, but the one to do the actual work has to be you.

The ones who stayed

There were people who stayed with me throughout the whole experience until now. Some are friends I had before it all happened, some are family, and some are new friends I didn't know before Paul completed suicide. They are all an integral part of my life and my healing. I treasure them all.

There are friends who stayed with me until a certain time and then needed a break, and after the initial hurt of the possibility of losing another friendship, I understood that I couldn't stand in their way of looking out for themselves. I had to support their decision to step away from me and the situation I was in, to be a good, supporting friend to them.

I appreciate everyone who helped and is helping me get through this time in my life. This new flexibility in friendships has been a good thing for me in that I am better at accepting new friends and am not completely devastated when an old friend can't stay in my life with me anymore.

I must mention I do have friends who have been there for me in one way or another since Paul completed suicide, either texting, taking walks with me, helping me with my children, or doing something fun.

They have also supported me even if they disagree with a decision I've made for myself, and I know that if it ends up that I've made the wrong decision, they'll be there for me then too. They are still doing those things now, 11 months after Paul completed suicide. They have shown me what a true friendship looks like.

◇◇◇◇◇◇ Let me explain/It would be so helpful

I have learned a lesson which, up until now, I had a very difficult time understanding. It's that friends will come and go. I never wanted to believe that, because to me, friends are for life.

I thought if a friend needed to go, maybe we were never really friends to begin with. Now I have come to understand that some people do need to go off and do other things, be with other people, and let their friendship from me fade away. The friendship dwindles into this place of suspended animation where it can be picked up again if they choose, possibly just like it never faded away.

Only to me it wasn't as easy as that because during the "fade away" time it hurt to lose the companionship we shared as friends. It would be so helpful if people could just be honest, but I think they hesitate in being honest because they're afraid feelings might get hurt. Believe me, feelings already did get hurt! I have learned to be friends with people who want to be friends with me, and if I find myself with no one at any one time, I still have myself and my faith.

Friends or no friends, I'm still going to be okay. There are times when friends add to the grief of losing a loved one to suicide. When a person is living each day with anxiety, depression, grief, confusion, and a host of other emotions because of the death of a loved one to suicide, it is going to affect their communication skills whether they have trouble communicating on a regular basis or not.

If a friend has trouble dealing with the misunderstandings and confusion social situations bring at this difficult time, then it's better for both of you to take a break. Due to the complicated grief one experiences in being a survivor of suicide loss diagnosed with AS, it will take an understanding and dedicated friend to stay with you through the whole experience.

If you have a friend in your life who can do this, it's a blessing, and I encourage you to hold that friend in your heart as a treasure. If you have a friend who needs a break from your way of communicating, I would suggest not holding that against them. They did the best they could, and as their friend, the best thing to do for them is to let them go.

◇◇◇◇◇◇

The ones who left

There were friends who left at different times after Paul completed suicide. I had met several of my friends at my place of work. Five years ago I started teaching at a small private school for students with special needs. The staff there consisted of five amazing people and myself. Over the years I had been at the school, the staff became like family to me. Each person there was very special in their own way, and I really tried hard to be a friend to each of them. There was one friend there, Carla, who I could talk to about things that were really important to me, I could ask questions about friendships, and also process different social situations that came up every now and then that I didn't understand.

As a staff we all appreciated each other and all cared very much about the students we were there to teach and support. We all worked so well together and respected each other to the point where we were a solid, successful team that brought real positive changes into the lives of our students. As friends, we were also there for each other to lend support when needed.

The school had become my safe place away from home. It was a place I was loved and accepted for who I was, and I felt supported and cared for by all of them.

◇◇◇◇◇◇ Let me explain/It would be so helpful

And then it was all gone. After my husband completed suicide, the school that had become my safe place away from home no longer existed for me. Now it was a place that had become awkward, some staff members didn't talk to me like they did before, and I was lonely and uncomfortable at the school.

There ended up being two friends from the school who have remained a part of my life. Both of them have been supportive since my husband's death, and I appreciate them more than I could ever express in words. They are like family to me. One of them is my dear friend, Carla, who has been there for me when I needed someone to listen, when I needed encouragement, when I wasn't sure how to help myself, and when I was in places so emotionally low I couldn't find my way out alone.

The other person, Josh, is someone I've come to think of affectionately as my brother. He is supportive not only to me, but to my two youngest boys as well. He has been the male role model in their lives for the whole five years I was at the school, and even now, when we are no longer there. I have been so grateful to have him in my life and in the lives of my boys.

In the aftermath of losing a loved one to suicide there becomes a new normal. It's a new normal that includes losing old friends and welcoming new friends into your life. It would be very helpful to a person with AS to try to be as flexible as possible with all the changes that take place with the new normal. I would suggest not fighting it. It is an exercise in futility to try to keep everything as it was before the suicide, and you can't do it because you have no control over many of the things that change.

The best thing you can do for yourself is to be willing to accept the onslaught of changes, new experiences, loss of relationships, and to let strangers help you in your time of need. As a genuinely quiet, private person, letting strangers help was very difficult for me, but I tried to be flexible, and I'm happy to say that most of the strangers who helped me are now my friends.

◇◇◇◇◇◇

Disconnections

Feeling disconnected is not conducive to emotional healing. As I became more and more disconnected to the people in my life, I felt more and more alone. I was not expecting the awkwardness that came with me just being in the same room with some people. I could sense their hesitation to talk to me. They didn't know what to say. I didn't know what to say. The loss of the closeness we once felt towards each other was confusing and unbearable at times.

They were all still physically there, so I felt some hope that things could go back to normal until I understood things were never going back to normal. My life had completely changed. There was no part of my life that wasn't touched by the suicide of my husband. My safe place away from home was gone. I had worked so hard to make connections with people, yet one horrible incident in my life left me feeling disconnected from those very same people.

I learned that I couldn't count on those relationships I thought were solid and secure. The relationships ended up being crushed under the weight of my husband's completed suicide. It seemed that the only thing I could count on was change.

Try to imagine something in your life that makes you feel very uncomfortable, such as going to a crowded place with lots of noise. Then the worst experience you could imagine happens and leaves you reeling from the impact it has on your life, where nothing is the same. The only constant you have left is finding yourself in a crowded place with lots of noise over and over and over again. Every time you turn around there's another noisy, crowded place you have to work your way through.

Change was my noisy, crowded place.

◇◇◇◇◇◇ Let me explain/It would be so helpful

The anxiety I felt over the loss of these relationships was intense. I had a constant stomach ache for over three months. I had no idea what to do about these relationships, and when I tried to talk to them, it was just pure awkwardness and never felt any better.

I felt I had other people to grieve over besides my husband. I was truly lost and felt completely alone, even though I really wasn't alone. The emptiness I felt inside was consuming me as I went about my days, mechanically doing what needed to be done. The nights were especially lonely and empty. I would remember the closeness I felt as we worked together as a team. I would remember the safety and support I used to feel at the school.

I was isolated in the middle of a busy city. Life was going on all around me, but I didn't feel like I belonged anywhere or with anyone. I'm having a difficult time right now finding the right words to capture the emptiness of my life at that time.

Change became the constant in my life. I could count on change happening in every area of my life on a regular basis. I was even going through many changes in how I saw the world. It would've been helpful for me to have been more willing to accept the changes that were happening instead of trying to fight them. One way I could've done that was to let go of what hurt in my life. If I had been more willing to let go and accept the changes in relationships, as part of the whole package of being a survivor of suicide loss, it would have hurt a lot less.

One thing I have learned is that letting go is sometimes the best way to handle a situation involving friends. I still think friends are for life, but I have come to realize that if the other person doesn't want to be in the friendship, the best way to move forward is to let them go.

One constant in my life was my children, and I was so happy I had them all. I've made it as far as I have because of the love and dedication I feel towards my children. I strongly felt I had to show them how to get through a devastating situation by leading the way. I had to be strong for them so they would feel secure even after losing one parent.

The connection I had with my two adult children was such that we supported each other. How wonderful it was to have them be so strong and capable. For the first time since they were born, our roles blurred together as the mother/child lines crossed into friendship.

◇◇◇◇◇◇

So many relationships lost

And so, throughout the summer and into the fall, I lost the fellowship and friendship of the people in my life I never thought I'd lose. While some did just fade away, there were others that ended badly as I received messages of harsh judgment, questions about why I wasn't glad Paul was dead, and faced the scrutiny of other people's timelines for my grief.

I was stunned. I just couldn't understand why the negative messages came at a time when I needed support more than I'd ever needed it. While I think the messages came from a place of care and support from the people who gave them, they were still distressing to me, although I have since learned there can be no expectations of other people, no matter how well I know them.

Losing close friends is something that every survivor of suicide loss I've talked to has experienced. The extra special difficulty this brought to me was that these people were close friends, and it had taken me the five years at the school to make, develop, and keep the relationships. As they were slipping out of my life I knew I didn't have the capabilities at that time to start the hard work of developing new friendships. The loss was all consuming to me, and left me feeling like I was in an abyss of loneliness.

◇◇◇◇◇◇ Let me explain/It would be so helpful

I still do not understand why my husband's death by suicide would reflect so deeply on relationships I had outside of my life with him. I have always thought his life or death should not have had any effect on the relationships in my life, but it did.

For some unfathomable reason I lost precious friendships in the aftermath of my husband's suicide. Why? What did the two have to do with each other? I got to a place where I wondered who would be the next person to leave my life when I needed them more than ever before.

If I let my thoughts wander on their own, I could over-think conversations, texts, phone calls, and emails, and be absolutely sure who the next person would be to leave me. So I had to concentrate and train my mind to think positive thoughts about the people who were in my life. I learned to count the blessings I did have instead of grieving over relationships I had lost.

It was helpful when I paid attention to all the blessings in my life because I slowly started to feel stronger and more capable of handling the losses.

◇◇◇◇◇◇

Chapter Four
Support

I need support—I can't do this alone

During the time after Paul completed suicide, I needed support from my family and friends more than I ever had before. Up until this time in my life I was usually able to handle any troubles I had by myself. This time, I couldn't just rely on myself anymore; I needed support.

I had solid, experienced, loving support from my friend Carla (a specialist in supporting survivors of suicide loss) for the first month after my husband completed suicide. She spent a lot of time with me helping with the finances, making sure I kept hydrated, eating healthily, getting rest, telling me what I was feeling was normal, and just being there. Then, of course, Carla had to go back to her own life, her own family, and her own new career path. I understood, but to be honest, I wasn't ready for her to leave. I was nervous to be on my own for the first time in 29 years, but it was the best thing she could've done for me.

So my support changed. It lessened. She was always there when I texted her, but I had started to count on myself more and more. I was very lonely at this time of my journey. My friends were changing although I didn't want them to; strangers were helping me instead of my friends.

For example, the people from our neighborhood wanted to do something to help me and they asked what I needed. I told them I really needed help with my landscaping because I still lived two towns away and it would be difficult for me, Levi (12), and Gabriel (11) to take care of well.

Different people from the neighborhood signed up for seven weeks of lawn mowing! I tried to go up to the house on Saturday mornings to give a thank-you in person to whoever was mowing my lawn that day. I met several people who didn't know me at all, but were still helping me, a total stranger to them. We soon got to know each other better, and the neighborhood became a little smaller and friendlier.

I appreciated all the people who came into my life during that first summer and fall. I struggled to connect with the new people I met because usually I can't emotionally connect with people at least until I've gotten to know them much better and I've spent time with them. Even so, the strangers quickly became friends.

For instance, one of the people who mowed the lawn for me also introduced me to his wife and they invited us to their church. Since then, we have become friends, and I met some other friends at their church. It was all a bit out of my comfort zone, but I was able to work out my uncertainty in the new friendships, and speed up the process of getting to know people.

My dear friend Justine has been encouraging and supportive with texts, cards and even phone calls as I have worked through this time in my life. Her texts were amazingly accurate, and came on days when I was feeling alone in the world.

◇◇◇◇◇◇ Let me explain/It would be so helpful

For me, support from people was a challenge at times, both because some of my friends left my life, and strangers became a part of my life. As an adult with AS, it has always taken me a long time to get to know someone, and an even longer time for me to feel connected to them in a meaningful way.

The emotional connection can also wax and wane as the friendship evolves, whether I want it to or not. For example, I can want to feel a connection to someone, yet not feel it, and I haven't figured out how to make it happen just because I want it to.

So support from people has been difficult at times. I wanted friends I had been comfortable with to be there for me, but some chose to step out of my life. It was helpful when I was finally able to accept the change of friendships I had no control over.

One friend I lost was very close to me and to my boys. I had thought she was going to be a part of my life and the life of my boys always. I'm not completely sure what happened, but we are no longer friends, and it all fell apart in the months after Paul completed suicide.

The strangers I wasn't comfortable being with yet were there, offering their support and help. So I accepted the support that was offered, and became grateful to have the new people in my life.

The neighbors were so generous with their time in helping me mow the lawn and power wash where needed at the house. They were amazing, and I so appreciated each and every one of them. It was helpful that I was able to accept the support offered instead of withdrawing because I was uncomfortable.

This was a period of personal growth for me as I experienced pain when some of my friends were no longer in my life and awkwardness in allowing strangers into my private life to help me. Now I have a better understanding of how it works to not be so black and white with friendships, and that there's a lot of gray areas where people can be a part of my life in different degrees of friendship.

◇◇◇◇◇◇

Confusion about support

Confusion reigned as I tried to maneuver through the intricate social situations I found myself having to deal with day after day. As explained previously, when the support from friends suddenly disappeared and it was too awkward for them to be around me, I felt very alone and confused.

I am not the greatest at determining how much I can call, text, email, or meet friends for support, companionship, and help, so I erred on the side of caution. I didn't want to do anything to jeopardize the new friendships I had, especially when I wasn't exactly sure why the old friendships had ended so suddenly.

So I'd go days, sometimes even a week or two, without contacting anyone, yet needed a friend so much. One thing I did understand about social interacting was that I couldn't put all of my needs on just one or two people. It would've been too much for anyone.

I had my family, but they didn't know the whole story of what I had gone through and was going through, and I didn't have the energy to fill them in, although I did tell my mother and my sister Terri more and more as time went by.

What I'm trying to say is that I was alone a lot during a time when I needed to connect with people I knew cared for me. I was left to take up the support, encouragement, and help from strangers, who are now friends, but at the time were strangers. It was a difficult time for me because there was so much change and new relationships to manage when I had no energy or desire.

I was confused about how much to disclose to the new people who came into my life. I didn't know how much to rely on them, when to call them if I needed help, and even what to say to them because I hardly knew them. I felt like I was in a friendship no-man's land, a minefield, that there was a ticking bomb counting down, waiting for everything to blow up in my face. It was like I was tiptoeing on egg shells.

I made the conscious decision that it was better to be on my own than to take a chance on messing up a friendship. It was not a decision I was comfortable with because I still needed friends in my life, but I felt that keeping them in the long run was better for me than making a social mistake in my confusion and losing them.

In truth, I was never really alone. I had friends who texted me every so often and were always encouraging and took some of the loneliness away. I had family who kept in contact and my sister Terri even flew down and stayed with me a couple of times, which was comforting to me in so many ways. She was there for me to talk to, she was there for my boys to get to know her better, and she was and is very supportive of me and the decisions I make.

◇◇◇◇◇◇ **Let me explain/It would be so helpful**

And so, confusion reigned in my life. Relationships were suddenly lost, friendships that were comfortable before now felt awkward, strangers came into my life and helped me instead of friends who said they'd be there for me, and I didn't know how to handle any of it as it was happening. I felt like my life was collapsing all around me and I couldn't do anything to stop it. I was so stressed out most of the time I couldn't address these problems.

I was overwhelmed with all the changes in my life. Too many things were happening without my knowing why. I still don't completely know why, but I have come to understand that they happen to most people who have lost a loved one to suicide, divorce, sickness, or an accident.

Some people just don't know what to do when their friend is hurting, so they do nothing. It would be so helpful to be able to tell your family and friends how you are feeling. You will be making yourself vulnerable, but at least you are trying to make things better for yourself.

There's only so much I can understand about social situations, and I have come to accept that I will struggle with that for the rest of my life. I've always believed that if I tried hard enough, asked questions for clarification, read lots of books, and watched many social interactions in movies, that I would somehow catch on and be at least moderately proficient with social interactions. Now I understand there will be no concrete answers or lessons to learn that will help me understand more. No two social interactions are ever the same and so, for me, comprehending social situations is analogous to herding cats.

It has been helpful for me now that I understand my own limitations. I feel like I can relax a bit more, be easier on myself, and just do the best I can. Accepting my own limitations was not easy. I had to let go of the idea that I could understand if I just tried harder. I had to accept that while there were social nuances I could improve on and understand, there were also social limitations I had to accept.

I have also stopped trying to explain my social deficits to other people. Social interactions are so natural to most people; they can't understand the difficulties I face, especially when my knowledge of information seems to contradict my lack of understanding about social situations.

All I do, and I encourage anyone who can relate to my experiences to do this, is to be as open and as honest as possible and to hope for the best. Please remember that you are not responsible for the conclusions people come up with for the way you are interacting with them; some will be patient and understanding, some will think you are an attention seeker, and some will think you are being rude. They are responsible for their own conclusions. All you can do is accept the way they feel and then you have the choice to either continue trying to work through the social interaction or say your goodbyes and leave.

◇◇◇◇◇◇

Get my own support—where?

There was a time I brought up the lack of support I found myself dealing with to my doctor. He suggested that I go out and find new support. He was adamant that I could do it. He believed in my abilities when I was convinced I had none.

I wondered how one went about finding support as urgently as I needed it at the time. How do you even start? Do you advertise on social media? Do you search for a support group and go to a meeting hoping there will be someone there who would become supportive of you after meeting for just an hour? Do you tell acquaintances that some of your close friends have left you to go through the aftermath of being a survivor of suicide loss, and you need more friends now? I pondered the words of my trusted doctor to go find my own support, with trepidation of how to go about doing it.

As I thought about how I was going to get support for myself I came up with a couple of ideas.

I started going to a church. People at church are friendly, they usually come up to you to say hello, and there are activities for the boys and I to either help out or enjoy. There was still one complication, and that was there were too many people all at once for me. So I asked for support from one person, and I met Elaine. We started meeting weekly to talk, and she and I clicked right away. We had a lot in common, she was easy to talk to, and was very supportive of me.

Then I started to walk with one of my friends. I met a friend for coffee. I was taking the boys to a grief support group for kids, and I met some supportive people there.

I had the online support group I had joined about three months after Paul died. They were very caring and supportive. There were a couple of people I was messaging back and forth with outside of the support group as well.

I had the friends who I didn't lose continuing to care and give support when needed.

So that was enough for me, and I had done what I had thought I couldn't do. I learned that a huge detriment to what you feel you can accomplish can be your own limiting thoughts. I could've stayed alone thinking that I couldn't make friends fast enough to help with the support I needed, but I didn't.

Also, I learned something interesting. I don't have to meet someone, go through all the formalities and stages of becoming friends before I can talk to them and get support. With the lady from the church, Elaine, I had support right away. She was on my side in anything I needed help with, which was just having someone to talk to most of the time. It was soon after meeting the ladies from the place where the boys had their support groups that I had some validation of my feelings from people who were going through grief too, which was important to me.

In the end, I did get more support, and I did get it myself. It can be done!

◇◇◇◇◇◇ Let me explain/It would be so helpful

I thought meeting people was arbitrary. When I went to new places, started new jobs, or moved to new neighborhoods, and I met someone and became friends, I considered it happenstance. I had never taken the initiative to deliberately go out and find friendship and support, like my doctor had suggested I do.

As soon as I figured out some things to try, I started to get positive results. The more I succeeded, the more

I was willing to accept I could get support for myself. I started taking more personal risks and allowed myself to be vulnerable to more people.

I became aware that not only could I get support for myself, but also that the support I got could be tailored to what was comfortable and safe according to my needs.

I also learned that support can come from many different places, people, and avenues. I had support that was face-to-face, online, in groups, and geared around working or playing.

Support went from something I hoped for to something I could make happen, and that was a wonderful feeling for me. I was on my way to being a bit more self-sufficient and socially competent.

What I was the most surprised about was how flexible support could really be when I was willing to try various kinds of support with different kinds of people. It was such an incredible feeling of accomplishment!

◇◇◇◇◇◇

The usual support doesn't work for me

Although I did successfully find my own support after my doctor's challenge, it was geared towards what was comfortable for me. The usual kind of support such as a formal grief group, going to talk to a therapist, leaning on family and friends, and opening myself up to be vulnerable to strangers helping out with private areas of my life doesn't *always* work for me.

I tried a couple of regular grief groups, but with each one I was uncomfortable sitting with a group of people

I didn't know and telling my story. Also, grief support groups are full of sadness and pain. I'd go to one and leave with more grief and sadness than I had when I got there. I would still have my own pain, and then seem to leave with everyone else's pain as well.

I wouldn't have enough energy to deal with their pain and my own pain at the same time. I wanted to help them, but couldn't even help myself.

There was also one grief support group I felt I didn't belong in because while I was dealing with horrible nightmares about my loved one because of the traumatic way we had found him, things that happened leading up to his completed suicide, and even my fears of the future, the others in the group would share their wonderful dreams of spending time with their loved one. They would say their dreams were like being with their loved one just like it was before they died. Their dreams would be comforting to them. I was glad for them, but honestly, it was hard to relate to them because my story was so different. And I didn't feel like I could share because my story was so different.

Leaning on family and friends was difficult at times because those people were emotionally involved, and emotions can sometimes cloud the way people see and respond to situations. In caring for me, they would sometimes say things that hurt. I know the words were coming from a place of love, but it was still difficult to hear what was being said.

Some of the things that would be said were about the length of grief—either I was moving through my grief too fast, or I was lingering in my grief when I should be over it—people also said how I should feel, such as feeling like I was glad Paul was gone. This was the worst one for me because it showed me the people who said it didn't understand me at all. I could never be glad anyone died, ever.

My family and friends would give me advice, which was fine, but if I decided their advice was wrong for me, I wouldn't hear from them for a while. I needed to make my own decisions, good or bad. I wished people didn't expect me to do what they thought I should do, and if I didn't, then get upset with me about it.

∞∞∞ Let me explain/It would be so helpful

Let me explain that I appreciated all the different varieties of help available to people struggling with the complicated grief that comes from a loved one completing suicide—the local support groups, online support groups, trauma therapists, friends, and family. I did try all of the different kinds of support. I found some to be more helpful than others. For me, one-on-one was the best, and most of the time I just needed to have someone to talk to who would really listen to me.

I didn't always need advice. I didn't always need a solution to my various problems. I just needed someone who cared enough to listen. It would be very helpful to just listen to a friend or loved one who wants to talk. I think it's pretty common to want to solve problems and give advice, and the person who is hurting may need that, but sometimes they just need to be heard.

Try asking your friend or loved one if they are looking for advice or a solution before giving one or the other. The only way I feel secure in a relationship is to have an open, honest dialogue. If I have to figure out if my friend or loved one is just saying something to be kind, or not hurt my feelings, or because they don't think I will be able to take what they're saying, it's just too difficult and confusing to me.

I wish the people in my life respected me enough to give advice, but then let me make my own decisions without the repercussion of them being upset with me. I had a lifetime of not being able to make decisions or having Paul be upset with me if I didn't do what he said.

After his death and the beginning of my new life, I very much needed to make the decisions for myself and my family with the support from the people in my life, whether they agreed with me or not, and to support me whether the decision I made was a good decision or a bad one. I wish we all could've been open and honest about the giving and taking of advice.

I need honesty, the kind of honesty most people have come to think of as impolite. But how are people able to discern "what's really being said" if they don't say what they really mean? This has been a mystery to me for a very long time.

◇◇◇◇◇◇

Lonely healing
Some days I found I couldn't do all the hard work of healing with other people. The reason is that with the grief, emotional pain, and depression I struggled with, there were days when any social interaction only added to the exhaustion and confusion. It made the hard work of being

proactive in my journey towards health and happiness much more difficult.

This quandary was painful. I didn't want to be by myself. I wanted to have other people in my life, people who could share their lives with me as I also shared mine with them. I needed people who I could care for and love. But it seemed at times like I just couldn't handle any kind of social interaction as I tried to move forward in healing emotionally.

There were times when I was actively trying to do things like deliberate mindfulness, positive self-talk, and art as an outlet, so that I could interact with others successfully, even though it still took a lot out of me.

Please let me be clear in saying that the reason it took a lot out of me and was difficult in any way had nothing to do with the person I was interacting with, and everything to do with me and my own struggles with socializing. Even social interactions with the most caring, supportive, and loving people in my life could be challenging.

I have found many times that I have had to choose between walking through this time by myself or having family and friends to walk through by my side. I have had to choose between healing and companionship. This was one of the most challenging aspects I have had to deal with in living with AS yet. How I have wished I could do both, but there were times I had to give up companionship and support to concentrate on healing.

I would text people, which would be a relief from the loneliness, or people would text me, which was not only a relief from the loneliness, but also confirmation that people were still thinking of me. I had my youngest children for companionship, but never for support. I made sure I was their support. I had my adult children for support and made sure they knew I was there for them too.

◇◇◇◇◇◇ Let me explain/It would be so helpful

I found the work needed to heal from the complicated grief of losing a loved one to suicide is a trial-by-fire exercise that seemed to take up every second of every minute of every hour of every day. The grief work had to be as relentless as the depression, anxiety, and grief I was healing from, or the hopelessness became overwhelming and I'd feel like I was drowning in it.

Interacting with people, even loving, caring, supportive people, can be exhausting, although it was something I very much wanted and needed. I felt the confusion, misunderstandings, and miscommunication of a conversation much deeper than usual.

I was not able to function at the level where I could handle social interactions, so it seemed every conversation left me feeling somewhat unnerved that I had said something wrong. There were times I had to choose between interacting with people and concentrating on doing the grief work that would bring me closer to health and healing. I could do both, but as the shock of Paul completing suicide wore off and the daily grind of living in the aftermath of his death was becoming overwhelming, I found I could only do one at a time.

Since I started practicing mindfulness, from the time I open my eyes in the morning until I close them back up at night, I'm trying to pay attention to my thoughts. If I catch myself thinking about the past or the future, I bring myself back to the present. Then I have to examine what I'm feeling. Whatever emotion I discover I'm feeling, I have to stop and feel it.

Throughout the day I try to embrace whatever emotion is filling my heart at any one moment, and most of the time it's an emotion I would usually squelch and stuff as far back into the recesses of my mind as I could get it, although with mindfulness it's different—emotions are felt in the moment instead of being stuffed back into the closet of your mind. They are felt as they come, and some days I need a break from the many that come, and some days I'm able to manage feeling them as they come.

It would be very helpful to have a plan for the day on what will happen if your grief, anxiety, or emotions are too overwhelming, a plan such as, when you realize you're starting to feel overwhelmed, take the time to do something you like to do if you can.

Other suggestions are: if you're someplace where you can't take the time to do a relaxing activity, you can bring your thoughts back to the present by thinking of something that is calming, or try to get home to start a relaxing, healing activity. Also, whether you're working or playing, deliberately do each step of the task or activity with all your attention focused on what you are doing. This will keep you in the moment and help lessen the overwhelming emotions.

It is important to continue working towards health and healing. It's also very important to be able to communicate and interact with the people in your life. If a break from being with others is needed, I would encourage you to take that break, but also keep in mind to have some time set aside to stay in touch with your friends and family.

◇◇◇◇◇◇

Support wrap up

Support, like friendships, can change over time. The type of support, the amount, and the intensity I needed kept changing as I gained more understanding of what was happening in my life and had more skills to cope.

I just didn't have the knowledge, practice, or experience to handle all the issues at once. At times it seemed like every area of my life had something going on that needed my immediate attention, while all I wanted to do was go to sleep with the covers over my head to shut the world out.

I had to triage support. I had to get support for what was troubling me the most at any one time as I walked through the aftermath of Paul completing suicide. For example, trauma support was at the top of the list at one time, and then depression and anxiety, and then relationships and the loss thereof, and eventually finances, the maintenance of my home, and grief for the boys and me.

As my support needs changed according to what I needed help with the most, the other areas of my life were still challenging. There are ways I tried to make life a little bit easier for myself. After the first few weeks of making the dreaded phone calls, I tried to relax and enjoy them. Okay, I have to be honest and admit I never did get to a place where I enjoyed them, but eventually I didn't dread them as much either! I also tried to be more flexible with the new friendships, and again, tried is the key word here. When I was in the middle of figuring out the finances, I wished I had learned more about the subject before I needed to be proficient in it, but I did slowly learn as I went along.

It was important to me that I keep trying, whether I succeeded or not.

◇◇◇◇◇◇ Let me explain/It would be so helpful

The type, amount, and length of support needed is different for everyone. You have to let your needs be made known to the people in your life, and if there's no one in your life you feel comfortable sharing your needs with, reach out to the resources in your local area. There are churches, support groups, and local mental/medical health facilities that can help. You can call the national suicide hotline for help in finding resources too. There will always be someone who can help; you just may have to be creative.

There will come a time when the level and amount of support changes. It will lessen as you become stronger, even if you don't feel stronger. The professional people helping you may encourage you to get more of your own support because ultimately, that's the goal, to be able to express your needs and get supportive help by yourself.

Therefore, it would be so helpful to always try new things even if it means going out of your comfort zone. The more new experiences you have, the more skills you will have to rely on when you need it the most. So don't shy away from things you've convinced yourself you can't do. Try just the opposite, and any chance you get go out of your comfort zone to learn new skills.

If there's something you know you don't understand and are not good at, take a course on it, or research whatever it is by yourself so you know more about it before you need to actually be proficient in it because life has decided you need to have practice in that particular skill. I guess what I'm saying is, be as proactive as you can to learn everything you can about things you have no clue about.

I have wished over and over again that I had learned more about finances before I had to make important decisions for my future and the future of my family. It is difficult for me to retain information I am not interested in, although topics I am interested in I absorb like a sponge and never forget. I have never been interested in business, finances, or money in general, which ended up being what I needed the most support in on the business end of my struggles in the aftermath of Paul's suicide.

I believe the most important thing is to keep trying and not give up.

Chapter Five

Sensory Issues and Emotions

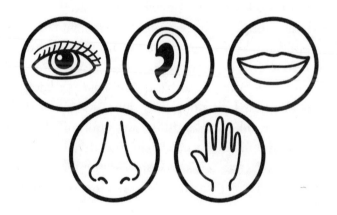

What did you say?

I'd be with someone having a conversation and I could see their lips move and hear sounds, but I couldn't tell what they were saying. Consequently, I couldn't remember a lot of what was said to me.

There were times after I texted people and they'd refer back to the text, but I would sincerely not remember writing or sending it. Once, a friend had to show me the text before I believed her, because I just absolutely had no recollection of texting her. As I read the text she showed me, it was as if someone else had written it until I finally recognized one part of the message.

I knew I was having trouble with my memory. It felt odd to know my brain wasn't keeping up with what was happening in my life. I depended on logical thinking all day every day. I was usually thinking about several previous conversations I'd had with different people to process what was talked about so I could determine if I had said something wrong.

I would also be thinking about what I needed to do, the order I needed to do it in, something I just read that was interesting, something I just read that I didn't understand, how to parent as I go along, and solutions to any current problems. I think, think, think, and think all day long. Knowing my memory wasn't right and that I wasn't able to think clearly was actually scary to me. The navigation instrument that steers me through my life was not working up to par.

One of the areas I had much more of a problem with than normal was word retrieval. I'd be searching my mind for a word that I knew I used all the time. My kids started to try to help by saying words that might fit in with what I had been saying. Eventually we made it into a game to see who could find the right word first.

There were so many thoughts swirling around in my brain that I had trouble making sense of anything. Luckily for me, my friend Carla remembered more about my life than I did, and at times could fill me in on conversations I didn't remember, phone calls I needed to make, and in general, things I needed to accomplish.

I had to write everything down. What I found very interesting was when I went back through the notebook, there were notes written by me containing information I thought I still had to get, and while it was a relief that I already had it, it was also kind of scary since I didn't remember getting it. I felt like I was walking around encased in a bubble with an impenetrable shell that kept out information and stopped me from communicating effectively.

◇◇◇◇◇◇ **Let me explain/It would be so helpful**

The decrease in my ability to understand what people were saying (recessive language) and the decrease in my ability to communicate to others what I wanted to say (expressive language) was a hindrance to everything I was trying to accomplish.

The expressive language deficit hindered my ability to communicate. It's a normal part of my life to be misunderstood and also to misunderstand other people and situations. During the time after my husband's suicide I really felt confused and misunderstood. I simply could not communicate even in the rudimentary way I've come to accept as part of my life with AS.

There were times when I just could not figure out what people were saying to me. I knew the words they were saying, but I just couldn't put them together in a way that made any sense to me. It was awful for me to realize my brain wasn't working the way I was used to it working.

And then there were times when I couldn't say what I wanted to say because all the words in my head were jumbled up and I couldn't put them together to make a coherent sentence. Many times I couldn't even formulate the thoughts required to begin to express myself coherently.

Sometimes the thoughts were so jumbled up in my mind nothing would come out when I tried to talk. The words were so bottlenecked it was like trying to get all the cars on a super highway through one open lane. It was frustrating, especially during the times when I actually knew what I wanted to say, but couldn't get the words from my brain to my mouth. And even if I could do that, I probably wouldn't remember what I was going to say!

Another area I was having difficulty in was finding the words I wanted to say when I wanted to say them, which is called word retrieval. These problems got much worse as I was working through the grief and trauma of finding my husband a few days after he completed suicide. I have had these deficits all along, but they got magnitudes worse after the night we found him. I was having so much difficulty with word retrieval that my kids started to automatically help me find the word I wanted to say. They did help as we went through all the possible words that fit the context of what I was trying to say.

My memory wasn't working very well. I had to write everything down, which was another cause of anxiety for me. I was anxious about forgetting to pay a bill, anxious about processing conversations because I wasn't sure I was remembering everything, and anxious that I was missing something important I needed to know. This was all even after I used the calendar on my phone to keep track of important information, but still, I didn't trust myself to have entered everything onto the calendar.

It would be helpful if family, friends, first responders, therapists, and anyone working with a person diagnosed with AS could understand all these struggles I just described, and be aware of the communication limitations.

◇◇◇◇◇◇

Anxiety

When I'm anxious I usually appear calm on the outside. While I'm presenting as calm on the outside, my insides can be a place where chaos reigns. My insides can feel nervous, uncomfortable, tense, and my stomach hurts.

When my anxiety gets high enough, I start to cry and it's difficult to stop. My whole world feels wrong and full of impending doom. Anxiety makes everything more difficult. It's hard to concentrate while making decisions. Dealing with anxiety has left me paralyzed when I needed to be able to think clearly and make wise decisions.

Anxiety is ever-present and intrudes on every aspect of my life. I wake up and have to start convincing myself everything is okay even before I get out of bed because of the sense of impending doom.

There are times throughout the day when I find my breathing has quickened, I feel panicky and notice I've let my anxiety get too high without realizing it. It's then that I have to stop what I'm doing and consciously breathe, think good thoughts, and convince myself what I'm suddenly afraid of isn't really happening. These episodes happen several times a day, and can even happen on good days.

Then, during the night, I can wake up in a full-blown panic attack, which in the middle of the night is just downright scary. My heart feels like it's pumping out of my chest and I can hear it in my ears. It's very difficult to downplay my fears in the middle of the night. After that, falling back to sleep just does not happen easily.

◇◇◇◇◇ Let me explain/It would be so helpful

I live with anxiety. It's just a part of my life and has been for as long as I can remember. I can have physical and emotional symptoms when my anxiety gets too high. Anxiety can make everything seem hopeless and there's a sense of impending doom that is so real, I have to remind myself over and over again there's nothing bad happening.

Anxiety makes it difficult to make wise decisions. It also makes communicating difficult because it tends to distort the meaning behind other people's words. It would be very helpful to be able to control the anxiety people diagnosed with AS live with daily.

There are several ways I've used to bring my level of anxiety to a more comfortable place. One is mindfulness, which is paying attention to the moment you are in, and feeling your feelings right then as they are happening. Mindfulness can bring your anxiety level down by coming to the realization that there is nothing happening to cause the feeling of impending doom.

Mindfulness can also help you relax and really look at what you're feeling. It is sometimes a surprise to find out the jumbled-up feelings that seem so out of control is actually just one emotion feeling out of control. Once that feeling is validated and you deal with it at that moment, by either writing about it, expressing the feeling through drawing, dancing the feeling away, exercising until the feeling is gone, or accepting it as part of the healing process, the feeling is reduced to a more comfortable level.

◇◇◇◇◇◇

Emotions

I used to be able to thoughtfully remove myself from the emotional distress of a difficult situation if needed. I used to be able to suppress my emotions and do what needed to be done without the complication of feeling those emotions. Now, since Paul died, it's difficult for me to sort out my emotions, which is why I try to count more on my intellect than on my emotions. Unfortunately, intellect doesn't always work because reason and emotions are diametrically opposed, and it's like reading a book on Calculus to find out why you're crying.

I've read that healing from grief requires relentless attention to your emotions. The purpose is to feel those emotions instead of stuffing them away or disassociating from them. One problem I run into is determining what emotion I'm feeling at any certain time. It gets much harder for me to discern which emotion I'm feeling if I'm experiencing more than one at a time.

For example, there was the day I opened one of the garage doors to try to get a lawn mower and the door hit a shelf put there by one of the people painting my home. The hit caused a computer monitor to fall onto my leg and then smash into pieces on the garage floor. Between the pain I felt where the monitor hit my leg, the smashed monitor lying on the garage floor, the shelf being in the way, and the reason I opened the door in the first place, I was suddenly chock full of emotions.

I found myself completely overwhelmed with emotions such as pain, frustration, anger, grief, fear, vulnerability, and hopelessness all wrapped up in depression and anxiety. I had no idea what to do next.

I remember that I stood there for what seemed like a very long time, trying to get some semblance of control over what I was feeling inside. I couldn't, so I very calmly started to clean up the pieces of the monitor, which for some reason made me lose what little control I had, and I picked up a broom and just started hitting the floor where Paul had last been, shouting choice words at him.

When the broom broke I stopped and was very unnerved at what had just happened. I didn't understand any of it. I still had all kinds of emotions swirling around inside and I burst into tears, which felt very awkward for me. When the whole ordeal was over I felt as though I had been through the wringer. I was exhausted, I was confused, and I felt like I had failed on so many levels. So I got the lawn mower out and started it so my son and his friend could mow the lawn.

What happened that night in the garage was an excessive, albeit truthful, representation of what I go through trying to regulate my emotions when I feel overwhelmed by them. There were just too many strong emotions that I had trouble discerning what those emotions were, never mind trying to regulate them.

Handling my emotions is a work in progress just as healing from my grief is ongoing. I take one day at a time and do the best I can that day. There is no break for me to catch up to my emotions. I have to deal with everything I always deal with in spite of the condition of my heart and my mind.

◇◇◇◇◇◇ **Let me explain/It would be so helpful**

Emotions are foreign to me. I deal with life intellectually. I am so much more comfortable with reason and logic than I am with emotions. Yet since Paul completed suicide, there's been no reason or logic to this whole mess—there's only been emotions. Strong emotions that come seemingly out of nowhere stay with me, and leave me feeling like I'm overwhelmed and have no understanding of what's going on inside.

If I try to explain how I feel to someone, many times I can only say that I don't feel well inside. Even the words to describe my emotions are difficult for me to use to communicate with because I'm not comfortable with all the strong emotions I experience. The one thing

I've tried to do since all these emotions have come into play is to try to tame them with meditation, practicing mindfulness, listening to music, talking to someone, taking a walk, or writing. I have also tried going to sleep, hoping that when I wake up the emotions will have calmed down.

In spite of all the effort of trying new ways to calm my emotions, sometimes it becomes a waiting game. I don't like the times it's a waiting game because I have to feel the emotions until they calm down and go away. The good part of the waiting game is, after the time spent feeling the emotions, they are either much easier for me to understand or have calmed down to a level where I can accept them a bit better and can recognize them faster in the future because of the time I spent being aware of them.

◇◇◇◇◇◇

Chapter Six

Strengths

Strength

Rules

I can bind myself to my own rules, which make sense to me, just as I am bound by the rules of society, which most of the time make no sense to me. I tend to be a bit rigid in following rules which, for me, make the world a bit more structured and easier to understand. I usually make rules for myself that I consider unbreakable. If I am in the right frame of mind to use this strength I have, I will put rules into place that help me to be successful.

For example, if I tell myself there will be no more negative self-talk, there will be no more negative self-talk. This might sound too easy, and that's true! Remember I said I can use this strength if I'm in the right frame of mind? Getting there is the difficult part.

I will not listen to my personal rules if I'm in a place where the hopelessness, depression, and anxiety are so high that they are in control, not me. If I find myself breaking a rule I've set for myself over and over again, I will set a smaller rule.

For example, using the negative self-talk again, I might make a rule to stop the negative self-talk if I *catch* myself talking that way. The rule is easier to keep, is not so black and white, and is still leading me in the right direction.

Rules are comforting to me in a world that is full of changes, unexpected surprises (good and bad), and very little social structure.

◇◇◇◇◇◇ **Let me explain/It would be so helpful**

It takes a lot of work to get to the place where this particular strength is helpful. If you also have this strength as a person with AS, a wise choice is to delve into doing what it will take to regain control over your emotions so you can start putting some rules into place to help you move forward. It may take some time, so don't get discouraged. Here are some things that have helped me.

The first is knowledge. Knowledge is power. If you understand what you are dealing with you can better help yourself to overcome it. Ask a professional for research-based peer-reviewed articles and read about depression, anxiety, and grief. Read about mindfulness to stay in the moment, writing to heal, art to express yourself, and meditation to stay calm. Arm yourself with the knowledge to fight for your own well-being. It will be worth it even if right now, as you are reading this, it seems impossible.

I was there, it did feel impossible, but what I wanted more was to be healthy, to live and laugh, and love my life. If you have knowledge of what you're struggling with I believe it will be easier to make the right rules to keep you on track towards health and healing.

The second is mindfulness. Honestly, when I was first told about mindfulness by my friend Carla I had absolutely no idea what she was talking about or how it would help me, and I had to decide if I was going to try something new that I didn't understand.

Thankfully, one of my pet peeves is a person asking for help and then not taking the help that is given. So I tried mindfulness and it worked wonderfully. I felt better! After a while I have stopped trying to find out how some of these things help because it seems like magic is in play. I have learned I don't have to understand something in order to benefit from it.

Instead, I just use the skills because they work. In using mindfulness I can get myself in the right frame of mind to use the strength of following rules I make for myself. I have come to understand this road of grief has a lot of twists, turns, back tracking, and falling, so the most important rule I have while traveling this road is: keep moving forward, and if I stop, I don't stop for long, and every time I fall, I get back up as fast as I can.

◇◇◇◇◇◇

Determination

As an adult with AS, I can look back at my life and recognize how I have had to be an overcomer for as long as I can remember. I have always known deep down inside that I was different from other people, not knowing how to connect with people my own age, being rejected, misunderstood, and always on the outside looking in at life had built up an inner strength and determination that I drew on to not give up.

There have been many times during this journey of grief where I've felt that inner strength get all used up. I felt exhausted emotionally, physically, and mentally. I was drained of energy, hope, and courage.

But if I went deeper inside of myself, I'd find more strength every time I thought it was all gone.

It was comforting to find out all my struggles had built up an inner strength that I could now draw on when I needed it.

◇◇◇◇◇◇ Let me explain/It would be so helpful

Growing up with AS in the 1970s was not easy. I knew I was different, but didn't understand why. It seemed as though my peers picked up on my differences too, but they probably didn't know why either. I just didn't fit in with other kids my age. I preferred talking with older people, and would visit a couple of elderly people on my street. I loved listening to their stories and talking to them.

Still, I yearned to fit in with my peers. It was lonely growing up without understanding how to communicate with kids my own age. I did a lot of watching to see what other kids did, but I never got the hang of it. What I did get was an inner strength to continue trying day after day to fit in and have friends.

It was that strength I drew on when I had a difficult time coping with my life after Paul completed suicide. Even when I felt I could not take any more losses in my life or one more day of grieving or another miscommunication with anyone, I would find the strength to handle more.

What I found helpful was reading inspirational quotes. The quotes were not something I would have chosen as helpful on my own. It was only after reading quotes on social media or quotes people sent me as encouragement that I found they helped me to feel better. Sometimes Carla would send me a quote late at night that I would smile at before falling asleep.

Another place I found determination was in the stories of people who had gone through very difficult situations and persevered their way through to better times. I either read the stories or watched movies about these people's lives. I saw how they would take each challenge on as if it was the only challenge they had at the time. It didn't matter to me if the stories were fiction or non-fiction, I still came away with more determination and inner strength.

My kids were always a factor in my determination to keep going. They needed the security of a parent who could be there for them and supply all their emotional, mental, and physical needs. Honestly, in my darkest, most difficult moments, it was the thought of my kids that would get me back on track, determined to keep going for them.

It doesn't always have to be children who motivate determination. A beloved pet, a spouse, a parent, a sibling, a profession, a cause, or close friends can also be motivating for a person to keep going through difficult times.

◇◇◇◇◇◇

Empathy

A common thought is that people on the spectrum feel little to no empathy for other people, but that's just speculation. I believe people on the spectrum feel the same empathy as neurotypical people, but they either don't know how to show it, or they show it in a different way that is hard for others to understand.

I care very much about people—while in the midst of the aftermath of my husband completing suicide I worried about the people who were also affected by his death.

My heart hurt for our children of course—their pain was my pain. I also hurt for his extended family and did what I could to help them.

The empathy I feel for others in a grief support group has, at times, been so intense I feel like I just can't stay in the group anymore, although I do because I want to help other people who are in grief.

One of the ways I help others now is to encourage the people who are part of the online support group I became a member of about three months after Paul died. When I go online and write encouraging, hopeful posts to people who are hurting just like I am, it helps me to feel better. I also receive encouraging posts from others who care and support me.

∞∞∞∞∞ Let me explain/It would be so helpful

Empathy is a strength people on the spectrum do have, like anyone else. I feel deeply about others, and love to help people when I can. I might not cry when everyone else normally would, or say sentimental words or phrases when it's socially expected, but I still care deeply.

I would encourage anyone on the spectrum to not feel badly or make excuses for why you might not show empathy like many other people. Be yourself without apology. Show empathy in your own way and at your own time.

I show empathy by trying to help the person who is struggling either by being there to listen to them talk out their troubles or sending texts, emails, and cards to show them I'm thinking about them.

There are times when I find the pain others are feeling becomes my own pain, and I can be more compassionate with them because I understand how much what they're going through hurts.

Helping others is a way to also help ourselves, because it feels so good inside to bring comfort to someone else who needs encouragement.

◇◇◇◇◇◇

Chapter Seven
A New Life

New address book

You know, some people buy a new address book because their old one is getting frayed around the edges, they've filled all the pages, or they've lost it. Then the people enter all the addresses of their friends into their new address book to make sure they can stay in contact with them.

I'm sure putting all those addresses of close friends and family into their new address books is comforting in a way because all the addresses show how many people they have in their lives who care about them.

As a survivor of suicide loss I found myself with a new address book and only had a few of the addresses of my friends left to put inside. This new address book isn't one I would've picked. I felt like I ended up with a lime green-colored one, which for me is not pleasant at all. I also felt like my new lime green address book had replaced a beloved lavender-colored address book, which for me was very pleasant and comforting.

I wasn't ready to let go of some of the addresses of my close friends, but they let go of me, so there was nothing I could do about that. Although I hadn't accepted the lime green address book yet, I had plenty of space in it for my new friends who came into my life and stayed.

Having a new address book is one of the saddest parts of living through the aftermath of the loss of a loved one to suicide. It's a strange phenomenon to have so much change in close relationships. I sometimes think the relationships weren't as strong as I thought they were all along.

I know the address book I explained above is a metaphor, but it's so close to the truth it might as well just represent the truth. I couldn't take the lime green-colored address book back and ask for another one. My beloved lavender-colored address book was taken away from me and replaced by one I didn't like, didn't ask for, and never wanted.

I had to learn to live with the lime-colored address book even though I absolutely abhorred it and the loss of friendships it stood for in my life. Change is hard during easy times, and this change was desperately hard.

◇◇◇◇◇◇ Let me explain/It would be so helpful

I wasn't prepared for the changes that came into my life at such a deep, personal level. My close friends who had never even met Paul became strangers, and strangers who had never even met me became friends, all because Paul made the decision to end his life.

◇◇◇◇◇◇

New normal

This new normal still doesn't feel normal at all. I feel like a fish out of water in my new life. There is so much of it I don't understand, and then there's the stuff I do understand but wish I didn't. Even so, in many ways I'm getting better at living in the new normal.

I still have important decisions to make, but now I have 11 months' experience under my belt. I am much more willing to use resources instead of feeling inadequate about not knowing enough to make good decisions. I'm also more capable in using the right resources and in trusting professionals to guide me in making wise decisions.

I've been trying to sell my house for seven months. I'm on my second contract with as many realtors.

There was a time during this second contract where I thought I had a rent-to-own deal with a couple who loved the house. My realtor warned me it might not be in my best interest. I was so hopeful it would work out because I really needed to move on out of my house and on with my life. I didn't want to give up the opportunity to have this couple move into my home with the rent-to-own situation. I hung all my hopes of ever selling the house and being able to move out on the deal this couple wanted to make with me.

Even so, I listened to my realtor and went to talk to a lawyer he suggested, who could give me more information about the deal. The lawyer was very knowledgeable and answered all my questions. When I left the lawyer's office I knew in my heart that it was not in my best interest to continue with the deal. My hopes were dashed, and it was a very difficult decision to tell the couple I could no longer offer them the rent-to-own deal. I may have made a huge mistake if I hadn't listened to my realtor and his lawyer friend. I was grateful to have them go the extra mile to help me make the best decision possible for my family and me.

In this new normal I'm a single parent, and although my main responsibility when Paul and I were married was to take care of the kids, he was still there on his good days to help. I find that I second-guess how I'm parenting because there's really no one to bounce ideas off of as I go. It's very helpful to have someone to talk over what might be the best for the boys. In my new normal my two adult children have helped with their own ideas and with feedback on my ideas.

I'm becoming more adept at taking care of my car, fixing things around the house, the upkeep of the landscaping, and the overall maintenance of the house. When I first moved back into the house after Paul died I was completely overwhelmed with taking care of everything myself. It's a nice change of pace for me to be successful and much more calm in managing everything that goes along with owning a big house, even if I do need help mowing the lawn every once in a while.

I know that I haven't explored this new normal enough to be able to relax, accept it, and live it fully. There are many things I still do exactly the same as I did before, when I could be changing things to a better way. Part of the reason is I forget I can do things differently, and because of my natural resistance to change.

◇◇◇◇◇ Let me explain/It would be so helpful

It was during the summer and into the fall when I felt so uncomfortable in the new normal that was my life. It felt like wearing clothes that didn't fit right, were the wrong color, and made of scratchy material.

I was so uncomfortable with the new normal mostly because nothing in it was normal yet. I felt inadequate taking care of the finances, with parenting children who were dealing with their own grief, with being a widow, with managing my own emotions and grief, and making important decisions.

Living in the new normal that comes with being a survivor of suicide loss is not a choice anyone gets to make. It just happens, and all that's left to do is to accept it. I still don't feel comfortable with the new normal that is my life, but I am getting better at living in it.

Time has helped me accept my new life. I've been living this way for 11 months now so I've had some experience with the new normal. I have a ways to go until I feel completely comfortable, but I'm getting there. If someone is just starting out on this journey or hasn't felt comfortable at all yet, I suggest giving the new normal some more time.

Another way to accept and comfortably live in the new normal is to try to make it your own. You can make it your own by the decisions you make, such as where you are going to live, what kind of car you drive, or even what you do on the weekends. The decisions can also be about smaller day-to-day activities such as when to have friends over, the way your family eats dinner, or how you celebrate birthdays.

Honestly, I resisted the changes my new life brought with it at first, but then I relented and accepted it wasn't going away. I knew I wouldn't be getting my old life back, so I had to make the best of the life I had. What I found was that it wasn't so bad.

Yes, I still miss the relationships I lost along the way, I'm still learning to manage my emotions, and I'm getting better at using resources to help me make good decisions. I also enjoy my new friends, have become comfortable using the skills I've learned to reduce anxiety and alleviate depression, and have found I'm starting to enjoy making decisions because I'm more confident with decision-making.

This is a personal issue where people should go at their own pace into their new normal.

◇◇◇◇◇◇

Who am I now?

I have the unique opportunity to remake myself into exactly who I want to be at this time in my life. I also have experience, wisdom, and knowledge to stay away from who

I don't want to be as a person. I am determined not to make the same mistakes I've made before.

There are many blessings I have enjoyed as I've walked and am walking through this journey of grief, anxiety, and depression. I have an inner strength that is greater than what I could have imagined before all this happened. I know now I can get through anything that happens to me in my life.

I also have many new skills to use for the rest of my life as situations come and go. I have learned to use mindfulness to keep me in the present instead of reliving the past or worrying about the future. I have learned to write and remove any toxic feelings, thoughts, or emotions from inside of myself where they fester and cause depression and bring me to a low place emotionally. I can use art to express what I'm feeling if I need another creative outlet. I have also learned to ask for help and not be stoic.

So who am I now? I'm someone who has faced a real-life nightmare. I've survived a horror that caused a level of emotional pain I didn't know existed, but I am someone who still wants to laugh, love, and be full of life!

I've endured the loss of several close friendships, yet I'm a loyal, kind friend to the people who are still in my life.

I've had to meander through hopelessly disorganized finances knowing very little about money, investments, 401Ks, IRAs, and other mysterious acronyms, and I'm a person who learned enough to be at least still financially afloat.

I lost the best teaching job I've ever had, because I couldn't do the job at the performance level I was comfortable with due to being overwhelmed by grief at the time. Then I got a teaching job I love, working online from home.

While these experiences don't define me completely, they have played a major part in molding me into who I am today.

◇◇◇◇◇◇ Let me explain/It would be so helpful

For the past 29 years I lost myself in a marriage where I was told what to like, who to be friends with, when I could go out with my friends, how to parent, what kind of car to drive, and even what kind of food to eat. I had to get all expenditures approved, be home when my husband was home, until I lost who I was and what I wanted in life.

Since my husband died I've had to figure out a lot of things, one of which is who I am going to be for the rest of my life. It's been too long for me to remember who I was before I married him, and from what I can remember of my high school and college years, I wouldn't choose to be that person anyway.

I have a clean slate to be anyone I want to be. What a unique opportunity for me to have a fresh start.

I'm going to start with who I've been since the night we found Paul had completed suicide. Since that night I've been a survivor, a learner, a mother, a friend, and daughter.

I can love and be kind in the face of rejection. I can manage the finances even when the finances are the most difficult thing for me to understand. I can have empathy and compassion for people who are hurting. I can ask for and accept help.

I can work, play, laugh, love, and look forward to the future me when I decide who I'm going to be.

◇◇◇◇◇◇

Chapter Eight
Time Goes On

Why does it still hurt?

It still hurts because I believe loving someone is total, complete, and 100% unconditional love. When that love is gone, like with my husband, I feel the loss of him as deeply as I loved him.

Honestly, I think it will always hurt to some degree. Hopefully it will be more manageable as time goes by. I have realized the grief will soften in time, but will probably never truly be over for me.

There are days I can remember him with a smile and it warms my heart, but there are other days I need time to grieve and cry to make it through. So many triggers bring back the pain from the night he was found, from both good and bad memories, and from some of the painful experiences we both went through as his illness got worse.

I also still hurt from the aftermath of his completing suicide, from the loss of relationships of people I was close to and even considered family, to being in an unorganized financial sink hole, to people judging me and expecting me to follow their timeline for my grief.

◇◇◇◇◇◇ **Let me explain/It would be so helpful**

Unconditional love is the only way I know how to love. I'm not very good at loving people in a gray area, where sometimes you love them and sometimes you don't. I guess black and white thinking does have its place in life, like loving someone, but it can also be detrimental when some flexibility is needed.

I expect this time in my life will always hurt to some degree, but like everyone else who has also experienced this kind of grief, I will find a way to live with the grief instead of fighting it.

It would be helpful to be allowed to share the grief I feel at any particular time with people I care about instead of having to keep it to myself.

◇◇◇◇◇◇

The grief timetable

First, let me share that although I have experienced grief many times before, I was not prepared for the grief that comes with the loss of a loved one by suicide. The grief was complicated. It wasn't like I could just miss him and be sad he was gone.

I also had feelings of anger towards Paul for completing suicide. I had to accept the horror of what he had done to himself. I had guilt to deal with because of how many different ways I came up with that his death was my fault. His death by suicide left me with a huge mess to clean up from in many ways, such as the bio-hazard clean-up so my home would be safe to live in, the financial mess that I had to figure out the best I could, and the emotional wreckage of the people who loved him.

With all the complications of grief caused by losing a loved one to suicide, there's no way to know when any one person will be finished grieving. Grief has no limits. There's no finish line. There can be no comparisons. Grieving people are as different as their fingerprints or DNA. No one judges anyone else about how different their fingerprints or DNA are to anyone else's. It is just as ridiculous to judge someone about the way they grieve, how long they grieve for, or the intensity of their grief.

◇◇◇◇◇◇ Let me explain/It would be so helpful

I have learned everyone grieves differently, and everyone's timetable for grief is different. No one should impose their own timetable on someone else's grief.

One person may withdraw to have time alone to heal, and some may need others around them all the time. There are those who like to cry with people around, and some who cry alone.

I'm sure there are people who keep themselves busy, as well as people who can't even work anymore. I can only speak for myself in saying that my grief continues to morph into many of those ways at different times.

So it would be very helpful to just be with a grieving person so they know they are not alone, and try not to make judgments about how they should be grieving.

◇◇◇◇◇◇

So many questions unanswered

One of the insidious aspects of being a survivor of suicide loss is not having answers to questions that are just burning to be discovered. The questions just ate away at me.

What was the last thing my husband thought? Did he know I still loved him? Why wouldn't he come to me for help? I reminded him every time I saw him that I wanted to help him if he'd let me. Was he scared? Why did he leave the house the way he did? Did he understand the devastation he would leave behind because his family loved him so much? Why would he leave this kind of legacy to his children? He wasn't a quitter, so when did things get so very bad and painful for him that he quit? He was a creative problem-solver, and while there was some creativity in his choice of the solution to his problem of pain, why didn't he think of a better way to help himself? Was there a way I could have stopped him from hurting himself? What if I had been there that night? Could I have talked him out of completing suicide? Should I have stayed with him so I was able to see how much he had deteriorated? What if I had called that night?

None of these questions have any answers. I have the choice to let these questions eat away at me, or to let them go and accept there will be no answers. I have to accept responsibility for my own actions and also let Paul take responsibility for his own actions.

I need to remember that if he wanted to complete suicide, he would have done so no matter what I said or did. The best way I handle these unanswered questions for myself is to know it's none of my business. That was the way Paul chose to handle his pain, his life, and his illness. He may have been in the middle of the biggest battle of his life, but in the end it was his choice to complete suicide.

I have always been at his side during the struggles he faced enduring life with a mental illness, and I would have been by his side at a moment's notice if he had let me. These are the truths I hold on to, the truths I have in place of the unanswered questions.

◇◇◇◇◇◇ Let me explain/It would be so helpful

I have always had to know the answers to questions I don't understand. If there's something I don't understand, I look it up. I look it up and read everything I can about the subject so I can understand. I have a craving to understand.

The unanswered questions left in the wake of my husband's suicide ate away at me. I searched the house and garage for clues. I thought I could find some clue to help me understand why he had killed himself. I thought I could find something to help me because I knew him so well. I believed he left something behind to answer some of the burning questions, even if he didn't mean to do it.

I was wrong. There were no answers, only questions. It would've been helpful if I could've accepted what happened at face value and not had a burning desire to understand and find reasons. Deep down inside I knew the reasons, but I didn't like them so I tried to find answers that better suited me.

It was an act of futility and a waste of time and energy. I should've trusted myself and what I knew to be true. At least now I do hold onto the truths as I believe them to be, and am able to let go of the unanswered questions.

◇◇◇◇◇◇

Moving forward

My journey to health and well-being is not done yet. I have stopped trying to bring myself back to who I was before this tragedy happened, which at one point was my goal. Now I've realized I want something else for myself, something better. I want to be a whole new person who has taken this time of brokenness and built a better life for myself and for my family.

What an amazing opportunity for a fresh start at this point in my life. So much has changed, and although I did my fair share in fighting that change tooth and nail, I am now glad that nothing looks the same anymore. The inevitable, unstoppable changes that go along with a new normal have given me a head start on making my life mine for the first time I can remember.

As I move forward I can honestly share that the most important thing I have learned from this journey is to love, forgive, appreciate, and take care of—myself. I have accepted that I am important; I'm worth the effort of using all the new skills I have, to be and to stay healthy.

I've learned that I make my own happiness and in doing so, I am in charge of how wonderful and full of life my days can be.

I have been given such a wonderful opportunity to support others in their walk towards freedom from the emotional pain of complicated grief because I've been there myself.

A blessing I've received from this journey is to not take one day for granted. I now live my life knowing each day is a gift. I am rich beyond measure because my treasure is time.

I now cherish every conversation, smile, hug, dream, text, and moment I have with each of my children with a new level of gratitude.

I am content because I enjoy the time I have to sit near the ocean, hike through the woods, watch the clouds, and enjoy the sounds of nature. The memories I make each day with friends, family, pets, and myself are treasures beyond words. My life is simple yet fulfilling. And most of all, my life is now mine.

As I move forward, I'm taking all this good stuff with me and leaving the ugliness behind, one step at a time.

∞∞∞∞∞ Let me explain/It would be so helpful

I'm not staying stagnant in this grief-filled, painful, anxiety-ruled, depressing place I've been in since Paul completed suicide. No, I am moving forward, even if it's just baby-steps at first, until I'm exactly where I want to be.

I have learned so much during this painful time of loss in my life. I've gone from barely functioning right after we found him to being pretty self-sufficient in my day-to-day life now.

The decisions I dreaded at first I now welcome as they come up, and this growth serves as another personal indication that I'm moving forward.

I have come to concentrate on the blessings in life that really matter, and am motivated to make them all a priority in my life instead of putting them on the back burner, only to be remembered if I happen to have a good day every once in a while.

∞∞∞∞∞

Where do I go from here?

I continue to work on healing. Even though I'm starting to realize the blessings that have come out of this dreadful time in my life, and am working on moving forward into a new life, I still have much to forgive, much to resolve, and many issues about my life to work through and heal.

I'm on a road towards gaining more skills, feeling better about myself, and being strong enough to handle any situation that comes my way. I have learned more about life, love, friendships, forgiveness, mental health, physical health, and loss than I thought possible in such a short time.

I have written, drawn, walked, pondered, listened to music, and whatever else helps me to get through this time of my life.

Now I feel like it's time to give back. It's time I helped someone else just starting on this journey to a new life because everything changes so drastically.

I take one day at a time to concentrate on the important things in life such as family, friends, me, my work, forgiveness, love, and gratitude.

◇◇◇◇◇◇ Let me explain/I would be so helpful

I would be kidding myself if I let myself believe everything is over now and I'm all healed up from the worst thing to have ever happened to me. It would be a mistake to stop working on my grief and the pain I still feel in Paul completing suicide. I still need to be using the skills I've learned to manage my anxiety and depression, maybe even more than ever, so I don't get complacent in my healing process.

I have a feeling that this could be a dangerous time for my goal of health and well-being because as I feel better, I might start thinking I don't need to work so hard for the life I want. It would be a grave mistake for me to think that way. Instead, I'm going to enjoy the progress I've made while still working just as hard, if not harder, to keep moving forward as I go towards a new life.

◇◇◇◇◇◇

Chapter Nine

Conclusion

This story is really only just beginning. I'm moving forward into the second year since my husband completed suicide with a firmer grasp of my new normal. I have one year's experience of living this new life and memories of my successes and failures to look back on as examples of what works and what doesn't. I'm making plans for my future instead of just going through the motions day after day.

I know there will still be grief work to do, obstacles to overcome, communication issues to resolve, but at least the new normal is starting to feel okay.

It's true, nothing ever stays the same, and it's a good thing because without change there's little chance to learn something new, but that doesn't mean change gets any easier. It's nice to know that it's worth it to accept change the best you can.

It may seem at times like hope is harder to hold on to as your grief waxes and wanes, but it gets easier as time goes by and there's always hope. After having a few great days where you feel good, are making progress, and things are looking up, don't be surprised to find yourself going through one of those dark nights of the soul again, where nothing is okay. It is normal in the grieving process to experience those ups and downs.

Remember, there are skills to use to help you during this time of grief and sorrow. And it's always a good idea to be proactive in learning new skills, even if something like this hasn't happened to you—just to be prepared in case it does.

You are your best friend, advocate, and caretaker. Try to be as prepared as you can to handle whatever sensory, emotional, mental, or relational difficulties you experience in life.

Help for Suicide Prevention, Intervention, and Postvention

For urgent or immediate crisis situations

- First and foremost, it is important to remain calm and be sure that you and those around you are safe. In the case of possible injury or direct threats of suicide, understand that intent of suicide is a potential medical emergency and help should be sought immediately. Be sure to remove yourself and others (particularly children) from physical proximity immediately. If possible, and when safe to do so, remove and secure any dangerous or lethal items that someone could use to harm themselves or others.

- For direct suicide threats or in the case of imminent danger, you should seek immediate help by calling your emergency response system (for example 911 in the US and Canada, 999 in the UK, or 000 in Australia) or, go to the closest emergency room or crisis intake center.

- If you are concerned for yourself or someone else who may be in suicidal or in emotional distress, you should:

  a) contact your doctor or a mental health professional, or

  b) contact one of the resources below depending on your country.

In the United States

National Suicide Prevention Lifeline: *www.suicidepreventionlifeline.org*
Tel: 1 800 273 8255 (call); 741 741 (text); 1 800 799 4889 (for those who are deaf, hard of hearing, or have speech disabilities)

Confidential, free support to those in crisis or emotional distress, 24/7.

In the UK

The Samaritans UK: *www.samaritans.org*
Tel: 116 123

The Samaritans helpline is available 24 hours a day for people experiencing feelings of distress or despair, including those which may lead to suicide.

Papyrus: *www.papyrus-uk.org*
Tel: 0 800 068 41 41 (call); 07786 209697 (text)

Working to prevent young suicide, Papyrus provides confidential advice and support for young people with thoughts of suicide, as well as anyone who is concerned about a young person who may be having thoughts of suicide through their helpline, HopeLineUK.

In Australia

The Samaritans Australia: *thesamaritans.org.au*
Tel: 135 242 (helpline); 1800 198 313 (youth helpline)

The Samaritans helpline is available 24 hours a day for people experiencing feelings of distress or despair, including those which may lead to suicide.

Lifeline: *www.lifeline.org.au*
Tel: 13 11 14

An organization with 24 hour crisis and suicide prevention support available to all Australians.

In Canada

Suicide Prevention Canada: *http://suicideprevention.ca*
Provides resources for local support throughout Canada.

Distress and Crisis Ontario: *dcontario.org*
Providing resources for each province, including phone numbers of crisis lines.

Further resources for suicide education and survivor support

American Association of Suicidology (AAS): *www.suicidology.org*
Tel: 1202 237 2280

Education and training, research, advocacy, resources, and survivor support services.

American Foundation for Suicide Prevention (AFSP): *www.AFSP.org*
Tel: 1 888 333 2377

Research, education, advocacy, and support for survivors of loss, as well as suicide attempts.

National Action Alliance for Suicide Prevention:
www.actionallianceforsuicideprevention.org
Tel: 1 202 572 3784

Championing suicide prevention as a national priority.

Parents of Suicides & Friends and Families of Suicides:
www.pos-ffos.com

Internet and email-based support for parents, families, and friends impacted by suicide loss.

Substance Abuse & Mental Health Services Administration (SAMHSA): *www.samhsa.gov*
Tel: 1 877 726 4727

Information and resources for suicide prevention programs.

Suicide Prevention Resource Center (SPRC): *www.SPRC.org*
Tel: 1 877 438 7772

Resource center devoted to the National Strategy for Suicide Prevention through technical assistance, training, and materials for suicide prevention.

The Compassionate Friends: *www.compassionatefriends.org*
Tel: 1 877 969 0010

Supporting families after the death of a child.

The Dougy Center: *www.dougy.org*
Tel: 1 866 775 5683

National Center for Grieving Children & Families, providing grief support for children, teens, young adults, and their families.

Tragedy Assistance Program for Survivors (TAPS): *www.TAPS.org*
Tel: 1 800 959 8277

National non-profit providing emotional support and survivor services for bereaved families of fallen military service members and veterans.

International resources

International Association for Suicide Prevention (IASP): *www.iasp.info*

Dedicated to preventing suicidal behavior, alleviating its efforts and providing a forum for academics, mental health professionals, crisis workers, volunteers and suicide survivors.

World Health Organization (WHO): *www.who.int/topics/suicide/en*

In more than 150 countries, WHO staff work side by side with governments and other partners to ensure the highest attainable level of health for all people.

The Salvation Army Suicide Prevention Services: *www.hopesalive.ca*

The Salvation Army is an international resource in many countries and oldest suicide prevention program (over 100 years of suicide prevention).

Suicide.org: *www.suicide.org*

A website that lists hotline call numbers for 62 countries around the world.

Websites for international hotlines

International Association for Suicide Prevention: http://www.iasp.info/resources/crisis_Centres

Befrienders: www.befrienders.org

Suicide.org: www.suicide.org

Index